The ManCode is an easy to read and u... W9-BTM-669 men, but contained in this message is a powerful and life-changing formula.

—RUDY NISWANGER, CENTER, KANSAS CITY CHIEFS (RETIRED)

This little book should be required reading for every man! I wish I had read it much earlier. It would have jump-started my spiritual life by twenty years. Every member of our staff and team will get a copy of it. Simply put, this book is AWESOME!

—JERRY MOORE, HEAD COACH, APPALACHIAN STATE UNIVERSITY,
THREE-TIME NATIONAL CHAMPION FOOTBALL TEAM,
LED ASU TO THE GREATEST UPSET IN HISTORY OF COLLEGE
FOOTBALL: ASU DEFEATED MICHIGAN, SEPTEMBER 4, 2007

The ManCode . . . it's like the *Tool Time* remedy for men from the inside out instead of the outside in. This book cracks "The Code" on what it takes to be what God planned for us as men instead of what the world says we should do to be real men.

—CAZ MCCASLIN, PRESIDENT, UPWARD UNLIMITED

The ManCode is a fresh word for men today. I love it because it is both biblical and challenging for men. If you are ready for spiritual adventure, climbing the mountain of greatness, get in this book and there is no telling what God may do with you. Read it. Buy it. Give it away. Men need this book today!

—DR. RONNIE W. FLOYD, SENIOR PASTOR, FIRST BAPTIST OF
SPRINGDALE AND THE CHURCH AT PINNACLE HILLS, ARKANSAS

So much of what takes place in churches today is fine as far as it goes, but it leaves many men cold and indifferent. There is a way to reach men and bring them to faith in Christ! Men need to take their place as followers of Jesus, and this book will certainly enhance that vital premise!

—DR. DAN BETZER, PASTOR,

FIRST ASSEMBLY OF GOD, FORT MYERS, FLORIDA

At times, men have a tendency to distance themselves from any type of relationship that goes beyond the surface. *The ManCode* describes not only the importance of taking relationships to a deeper, more intimate level but gives practical advice on how to be the man God intended us to be through those relationships.

—BRIAN CLINE, PRESIDENT, PASTOR APPRECIATION MINISTRIES

The ManCode unlocks the secret for men experiencing the life God intended. In this simple yet profound book, you will discover the five relationships God intended for every man to develop. This book is a must read for every man.

—DR. ROBERT JEFFRESS, PASTOR,

FIRST BAPTIST CHURCH, DALLAS, TEXAS

I love this book because it goes right to the heart of where men are. *The ManCode* unlocks the code that will help men reconnect. It shows how God designed us to live, work, play, and love in the atmosphere of healthy relationships.

—BILL DYE, SENIOR PASTOR,

NORTH MONROE BAPTIST CHURCH, LOUISIANA

All men—young or old, longtime Christians or newly committed Christians—will benefit from understanding the numbers in *The ManCode*.

—COACH DUTCH SCHROEDER, FORMER BASEBALL COACH AND
PROFESSOR, BAYLOR UNIVERSITY

The ManCode helps every man crack the code for living life at full capacity. I recommend this book to all my friends and practice the principles in my personal life!

—DR. MICHAEL D. MILLER, PRESIDENT
AND EXECUTIVE PUBLISHER, NAVPRESS.COM

The ManCode is a seemingly simple five-number set. But they have the potential to change the life of any man willing to spend the few hours it takes to read. Get ready to do some soul-searching.

—TROY DUNGAN, CHIEF WEATHER ANCHOR, RETIRED, WFAA-TV,
DALLAS–FORT WORTH, TEXAS

Downloading this practical and biblical code will not only challenge men, it will change men! Riveted to biblical principles, *The ManCode* systematically unlocks a relevant strategy for men, building high-impact relationships that make a difference for time and eternity.

—DR. KEITH THOMAS, SENIOR PASTOR,
COTTAGE HILLS BAPTIST CHURCH, MOBILE, ALABAMA

THE MAN CODE

UNLOCK THE SECRET

1-3-12-120-3000

DR. DENNIS SWANBERG
RON SMITH

WORTHY

Published by Worthy Publishing, a division of Worthy Media, Inc., 134 Franklin Road, Suite 200, Brentwood, Tennessee 37027.

HELPING PEOPLE EXPERIENCE THE HEART OF GOD

eBook available at worthypublishing.com

Library of Congress Control Number: 2012956459

For foreign and subsidiary rights, contact Riggins International Rights Services, Inc.; rigginsrights.com

ISBN: 978-1-61795-154-1 (trade paper)

Cover Design: Christopher Tobias
Interior Design and Typesetting: Bart Dawson

Printed in the United States of America

13 14 15 16 17 CHG 7 6 5 4 3 2 1

I want to dedicate this book to my two sons,
Chase and Cole.
My prayer is that they will see the code lived
out in my life on a daily basis.

—RON SMITH

I want to dedicate this book to my two sons,
Chad and Dusty,
and The Boys on The Bayou.

—DENNIS SWANBERG

CONTENTS

AUTHORS' NOTES

A NOTE FROM RON SMITH

In 2005, Dennis Swanberg and I sat down in a coffee shop at the Opryland Hotel in Nashville to discuss one of Dennis's ideas. Because I've been his manager for over a decade, and because Dennis has produced numerous videos, has hosted a cable television show, and has written several books, this brainstorming session was nothing new. Over the years, Swan and I have talked about hundreds of concepts, but this one was different. When Dennis began to share his thoughts, I could see that he was gripped by a level of passion—a sense of excitement and possibility—like I had never seen before.

Now, Dennis Swanberg is a pastor at heart, but he is also a very funny man. He has a natural gift for comedy, a gift that he has dedicated to the Lord. So it's no surprise that over the past ten years he has traveled the world over encouraging audiences with his humor and his insights. Because he remains a pastor first and foremost, Dennis's real purpose isn't hard to understand: Swan just wants to see people come to know the Lord. But it doesn't stop there.

Dennis also has a second passion, a second obsession that drives him to bounce out of bed in the morning. That second passion is men's ministries, and Dennis is *serious* about it. Swan believes that when good men are drawn to Christ, that when like-minded guys gather and reach out to one another and to their communities, miracles happen.

So on that day in Nashville, when Dennis began to describe a sequence of numbers that had been on his heart—numbers that, by the way, had a special significance for men—I knew he was wrapping his mind (and his heart) around a very important idea. Swan told me that if men could simply understand a short string of numbers—and if men could learn to live by them—their lives would be changed forever. Swan believed that if enough guys learned how to share these numbers, we would see a true change in our homes, in our churches, and in our culture. So I listened to Dennis for an hour or so, and I began to share his excitement. That's when a title jumped into my head: *The ManCode*. Dennis immediately agreed on that title, and we started working on the details.

Fast-forward two years. By this time, Dennis and I had worked through the basics of the ManCode, and we were ready to get serious about pulling everything together in a book. So we partnered with our friend Criswell Freeman, and we started to get our thoughts on paper. This short book is the umpteenth rewrite of the original text. Initially, we wrote a book that came in at a whopping 280 pages, but that seemed, at least to us, to be overkill for most guys. So we tried several other versions, shortening the text each time. Finally, we decided that we wanted you, the reader, to experience something like that very first conversation we had at Opryland, something you could easily digest in a couple of hours. We pray this little book truly offers you that opportunity, the opportunity to unlock a code that will change your life. We hope we've written it in a quick, easy-to-read style that won't make your eyes glaze over.

We know the ManCode works because we've seen it over and over again. So don't be surprised if you see that the ManCode is already working in your life and in the lives of those around you. I have to warn you: please don't read any further if you are not ready to see major changes in your life. The ManCode will challenge you in ways that you may not have been challenged before. The ManCode is simple, and it's easy to share, but it may not be quite so easy to implement, especially if you're a grizzled guy who's set in your ways. Once you understand how important these numbers are to you and your loved ones, I predict you'll buy into the ManCode and share it.

Are you man enough to learn and live the ManCode? I pray that you are!

A NOTE FROM DENNIS SWANBERG

It's a simple question but a tough one: Who's your best friend?

If you're like most guys, you may answer, "I've got lots of friends." But that answer may be a cop-out, because if you're like most men, you have an oversupply of skim-the-surface friendships and an undersupply of the genuine kind.

We men are *so* predictable. As a way of avoiding even the *remotest* possibility of intimacy, most of us are quick to form a complex web of surface-level relationships, an ever-expanding collection of buddies. Yet we never manage to develop even one *really* close friendship, and it doesn't stop there. When it comes to the most important relationship of all, the relationship that each of us chooses to establish with God, most of us are quick to *avoid* intimacy in that relationship too. That's where the ManCode comes in.

This book is about forming real (that is, intimate) relationships, starting with your relationship with the Creator of the universe and branching out from there. So the ManCode identifies an ever-expanding circle of connections, signified by this short string of numbers:

1 3 12 120 3000

The ManCode is deceptively simple, but I'm convinced it can be a powerful tool for you, a way to reorganize your thoughts and revolutionize your life. I believe that if you can master the relationships that are represented by these five numbers, you'll establish the right priorities, make the right plans, diagnose any unforeseen difficulties, make midcourse corrections, and achieve the kind of positive results that you desire and God intends.

So prepare to unlock a combination that never fails. We call it the ManCode, and we're confident that it's God's special code *for you*.

For where your
treasure is,
there your heart
will be also.

—

MATTHEW 6:21

INTRODUCTION

During World War II, both sides encrypted their messages and for good reason. Success on the battlefield depended on surprise, which meant that neither side wanted the other to know its plans.

Thankfully, our side was able to break the enemy's code first, so we knew exactly where the bad guys were headed and what they were up to. Military historians estimate that our code breakers shortened the war by several years and saved millions of lives. In short, those who broke the code won the war. The same applies to you.

If you want to win your personal struggles against your enemies—hopelessness, failure, and temptation—you need to break the code for successful living, and you need to break it now. This book offers you that code.

By gaining a clear understanding of the elements that comprise the ManCode—and by putting those principles into practice—you'll be prepared to win the personal battles that you face every day: battles of the heart and the mind in your world, in your workplace, and in your home. You already know how tough those struggles can be, and you know how important it is to win them. Don't worry: if you use the right tools—and if you have the right code— like the US military in World War II, you're destined for victory.

Here's a simple code that can change your life. It's a series of numbers called the ManCode: five numbers that describe the crucial relationships you need to unlock your potential and achieve *real* success. If you're a man who's leading a nearly perfect existence, a life free of foul-ups, bloopers, and blunders—and if you're clearly at peace with your path and your faith—then you've already cracked the code and you're already reaping the rewards. If you're like the rest of us, struggling from one day to the next, trying to do the right thing but often falling short (or down), then you need the ManCode, and you need it *today*.

To help visualize the code, think back on your teen-age years. Remember the combination lock on your high school locker? You needed the right numbers in the proper sequence—the code—in order to get inside. If you spun the lock's dial in just the right way, click! The tumblers fell into place, the lock opened, and you were in business. Like-wise, every man has a combination of numbers that, when applied in the proper order, can unlock his potential and revolutionize his life. This book is about your finding that combination and using it to discover who you are, where you're going, and what you're supposed to do when you get there.

Most men haven't come close to unlocking their personal codes. They are still hanging out in the same places, dealing with the same issues, making the same mistakes, suffering the same results, and living with the same regrets that have kept them tied up in knots for years. To make matters worse, far too many guys aren't at peace with their own particular situations. They believe, quite correctly, they could be contributing more to the world, and they'd like to receive more in return for their contributions, but they're not sure how to get there from here.

If you're such a man, if you're a guy who still has lots of room (and desire) for improvement, here's the combination—we've chosen to call it the ManCode—a string of five numbers that will unlock a world of opportunities for you:

1 3 12 120 3000

What do these numbers mean? To get things started, let's consider each part of the ManCode.

1

The first number of the ManCode is **1**. It signifies your need for a One-to-one relationship with God. This is the most important number in your code, and it is nonnegotiable. This number of the ManCode, like the being it describes, does not change—not today, not tomorrow, not ever.

Face it: you're hardwired for a relationship with something bigger than yourself. If you don't have it, that's why you're empty. If you don't have it, that's why you're miserable when it gets quiet. You can't stand to be alone with yourself because you weren't created to be alone. Whether you realize it or not, you possess a deep desire to experience a One-to-one connection with the Creator of the universe. God made you that way; it's simply part of who you are. It's woven into your DNA.

But if you're like most men, you discovered a long time ago that finding *lasting* fellowship with the Creator isn't easy. Why? Because you're not only wired to *need* a relationship with God, you're also hardwired to want things your own way. That means you're constantly tempted to *resist* God and to *rebel* against his laws (think about man's fall in the Garden of Eden). You're probably just a little too hardheaded, a little too fond of instant gratification for your own good. As a result, you probably have a tough time when it comes to the difficult job of obeying your Father. You're not alone. Everybody resists God at one time or another, and so will you. But as you mature, you should realize that when it comes to God's instructions, it's better to be teachable than headstrong.

Great athletes can be successful for a while with nothing more than raw talent. But in order to win consistently at the highest levels of competition, even the best players need great coaches. God is the ultimate coach. Are you coachable? Are you willing to listen to your Father and learn from him, or do you insist on doing things your way?

To crack the ManCode, you've got to decide who's in charge: you or God. Only you can determine whether you'll pay attention to the coach or not. Only you can decide whether you'll be a teachable man or a stubborn know-it-all. Only you can choose to be a team player on God's team or not. Of this you can be sure: if you want to be a winner in the truest sense of the word, you'll need to let God call the plays, which means you'll need to build a One-to-one relationship with him. That means letting God call the signals on every down.

3

The second number of the ManCode is 3, a number that signifies three friends you can trust completely. This number is negotiable. For you, the number might be 2, 3, or 4. Whatever the exact number is for you, keep the group small and make sure these guys are Christian men who will be there for you in good times and bad.

Every man needs a small group of Christian friends, a cadre of trusted counselors to watch his back, hold him accountable, and carry him when he can't carry himself. If there's a problem, these guys are available 24/7, no questions asked. But most men aren't comfortable with *really* close relationships like this. If you're one of those guys, get over it.

New Testament scholars point out that Jesus seems to have forged special relationships with three disciples: Peter, James, and John. These three men appear to be Christ's inner circle. What was good for Jesus is good for you and only more so. After all, Jesus was the Son of God. He was accountable only to the Father. But you're accountable to a wide range of people: family, friends, and coworkers, for starters.

In the last several years the word *accountability* has become very popular in Christian circles. Accountability to some means judgment; but here, it's simply assisting and encouraging one to be truthful to self, to God, and to significant others so that freedom and wholeness can become a reality. If you want to be a real success, make up your mind to hold yourself—and your closest confidants—accountable in the truest sense of the word.

The dictionary defines *accountability* as "the act of making a person responsible for his actions." That's exactly what your group of 3 should do for you. These three men should help you take inventory of your life: your victories and defeats, your strengths and shortcomings, your big plays and your boneheaded blunders. You should do the same for them. To have a 3, you must be a 3.

So even if you consider yourself a loner, remember that you still need a small group of high-octane comrades-in-arms—men who are as close to you as brothers, men who are firmly grounded in their relationship to God. These are the guys who know almost everything about you but love you anyway.

Real friendship between men, the kind of "right down there in the foxhole with you" mentality that we're describing here, is far less common than you might think, because most of us guys are more comfortable with surface-only friendships. We want to appear large and in charge, so we never express our deepest emotions to other men, not even to our closest friends. That's why most guys have lots of acquaintances but very few *close* friends. This causes big problems because all men (including you) need allies who are totally trustworthy, totally available, and totally supportive.

In selecting your own group of 3, you should look for guys who will *always* tell you the truth, no sugarcoating allowed. They should be men who are courageous enough to call you on the carpet when appropriate. They should know how to pump you up when you're down and how to celebrate your victories when you're up. Your group of 3 should be willing and able to help you handle your frustrations, your hurts, and your humiliations. These guys can also serve as emotional trash collectors by helping you dispose of any mental garbage you've managed to accumulate. These buddies are always on call, and your secrets are always safe with these rugged saints.

12

The next number in the ManCode is **12**, a number, by the way, that appears over and over again in the Bible. So if you were raised in and around a church, the number **12** should come as no surprise. When Jesus was looking for companions to share the load of his ministry, he chose a dozen men. Even *after* Christ ascended, the disciples quickly gathered and elected a twelfth man to take Judas's place.

In the ManCode, **12** is a negotiable number. Perhaps your large group will be numbered in single digits or maybe you'll have more than a dozen. The exact number isn't crucial, but the group itself *is* crucial. Even Jesus felt it was important to have a group of men to eat with, to fellowship with, and to travel with. Since it was good enough for him, it's good enough for you too.

This group of **12** is a larger collection of friends and supporters. Many but not necessarily all will share your Christian faith. (By the way, if you're worried about hanging out with non-Christians, remember that Jesus made himself available to saints and sinners alike—and if you're serious about leading nonbelievers to Christ, you probably can't do it while preaching to the choir.)

The **12** men who make up your larger group should be guys whose company you enjoy. They're guys you can golf with, fish with, travel with, and worship with. They offer friendship and fellowship, but it shouldn't stop there.

As your group of **12** grows, they will become more like your **3**: honest, confidential, and transparent. Like a rehab group finds community through open dialogue, sharing openly and wholly with your **12** will allow self acceptance and self actualization to occur. But make no mistake: the relationships you form in your group of **12** will be of little use to you *until* you have the numbers **1** and **3** firmly in place. It's back to the example of your high school lock combination: first **1**, then **3**, and then **12**.

But there's more.

120 and 3000

The number **120** stands for the church. You may attend a church that's much larger or significantly smaller than that, which is perfectly okay. But we've chosen the number **120** for a good reason. In the book of Acts, we are told that on the day before Pentecost about **120** believers gathered in an upper room in Jerusalem. This band of believers gave a jump start to the early church. Your participation in a local church can help jump-start your world too.

Now you may be thinking, *Here we go again. Another push to get me to go to church.* If you're thinking that, you're right. You need the church much more than the church needs you. And you need it right now!

The local church is at the heart of God's plan for *our* world *and* for *your* world. The church has all the spiritual gifts, human skills, and earthly tools it needs to accomplish God's will, so if you're serious about involving yourself in his master plan, you need to do so by throwing yourself into the work of his church.

In 1 Corinthians 3:16, Paul states that we believers *are* the church, but too many of us aren't behaving like it. Instead, too many of us (especially us guys) are watering down the importance of corporate worship. But God has other intentions! Of course your 3 and your 12 may be men outside of your church family, but the church is not to be excluded from your ManCode experience. God wants you involved in the 1, 3, 12 of his church—just as he wants the church to bless and influence your 12, 3, 1.

By the way, have you noticed the progression from 1 to 3 to 12 to 120? Can you understand how that progression might work for you? You begin with a One-to-one relationship with God. Then you expand your influence by finding (and keeping) three trusted friends, men who are rock-solid brothers in the faith. Next, you increase your influence with a robust group of buddies numbering about a dozen (or more). Then, as an active member of a church, you experience yet another multiplier effect. That's where the number 3000 comes in.

The last number of the ManCode is 3000. It's the number of men and women who responded to Peter's invitation to be baptized on the Day of Pentecost, so this number signifies the need to reach out to your community and to the world. It's a number that reminds us of the miraculous things that can occur when God works in the lives and hearts of his children and his churches.

Think of all the things that came after Pentecost: churches were built, fellowships were established among believers, mission trips were launched, lives were forever changed, and the good news was spread far and wide. The echoes of those great victories are still heard around the world today.

It's About Balancing Your Responsibilities

Your life is a balancing act, a tightrope walk with overcommitment on one side and undercommitment on the other. This old world has a way of gobbling up your time, and if you're not careful, you'll find yourself caught up in a web of trivial, low-priority pursuits. So it's important to think carefully about how you choose to prioritize your day *and* your life.

If you're a married man, you have a significant responsibility to your wife. God's Word is clear: you must care for your wife, you must love her as Christ loved his church, and you must never give her the leftovers of your time.

A Christ-centered marriage is an exercise in faith, love, understanding, forgiveness, and encouragement. It requires empathy, tenderness, patience, and perseverance.

A Christ-centered marriage also requires large helpings of common sense, common courtesy, and uncommon caring. Simply put, it takes time to be a good husband. It also takes lots of time to be a good dad.

If you're a father, you also have a responsibility to your kids. You're instructed to "train up a child in the way he should go" (Proverbs 22:6, NASB), and that doesn't happen by accident. Training young people takes patience and perseverance. Yet even if you're a doting dad and a devoted husband, you still have another responsibility: your friends.

In today's media-bloated world it's easier than ever to become a virtual hermit, a guy who cocoons himself comfortably inside the house, focusing on big screens, medium-sized screens, and pocket-sized screens. Please don't become a captive of your own man cave. Instead, take the time—and make the time—for your buddies. They'll be better for it, and so will you.

You're Always under Spiritual Attack

Whether you know it or not, you're always under spiritual attack. Temptation never takes a vacation, it never oversleeps, and it never phones in sick. You can choose to do the wrong thing, the dumb thing, the impulsive thing, or the immoral thing. If you allow those enticements to take hold of your life, you'll experience the inevitable hardships and heartbreaks that result when men behave badly.

But if you acknowledge the Lord in all your ways, you'll be directed toward a brighter path.

In his letter to Jewish Christians, Peter offered a stern warning: "Your adversary, the devil, prowls around like a roaring lion, seeking someone to devour" (1 Peter 5:8, NASB). What was true in New Testament times is equally true in our own. Darkness is indeed abroad in the world, and it continues to sow the seeds of destruction far and wide.

The English devotional writer Oswald Chambers correctly observed, "Our battles are first won or lost in the secret places of our will in God's presence, never in full view of the world." Chambers understood that life is a battleground, a place where good decisions—and their opposites—have consequences.

Your job, as a Christian man living in a dangerous world, is to recognize temptation and fight it. If you sincerely want to defend yourself against the spiritual attacks that threaten you and your loved ones, the ManCode can help. When you understand and implement all five numbers in the ManCode combination, you'll find yourself focusing on God's plan for your life, and you'll build a strong defense against potential spiritual snares.

The Slices of Your Life

The five numbers of the ManCode describe five slices of your life: your relationship with God, your relationship with a small group of spiritual mentors, your association with a larger group of close friends, your role in the church, and your willingness to become a part of the church's renewed outreach in the world. Each of these slices is vitally important to your spiritual health.

Your life unfolds day by day, hour by hour, moment by moment. Every waking moment you have choices to make: what to do, what to say, how to direct your thoughts. The choices you make have consequences: wise choices lead to victory and peace while unwise choices lead elsewhere.

Some decisions are easy to make because the consequences of those decisions are small. When the person behind the counter asks, "Want fries with that?" the necessary response requires little thought because the consequences of that decision are minor.

Some decisions, on the other hand, are big, *very big*. The biggest decision, of course, is one that far too many people ignore: the decision concerning God's only Son. But if you're a believer in Christ, you've already made *that* choice and you have already received God's gift of grace. Perhaps now you're asking yourself, "What's next, Lord?" If so, the ManCode will help you find your way.

Each number in the ManCode is intended to help

you make better choices by focusing on a single slice of life and deciding *in advance* how you will deal with that number. So please don't think of the ManCode as an abstract concept based on some theoretical reasoning. Think of the ManCode as five separate tools you can use to help manage five slices of your life. Once you unlock the Man-Code, you'll find it easier to make wise choices and harder to make dumb ones.

Think About Your Own Code

Throughout this book you'll be asked quite a few questions, all of which are intended to help you crystallize your thoughts and formalize your own personal code. You'll be asked to identify the names of the men in your group of **3** and in your group of **12**. Plus you'll be asked some straightforward questions about your life, your path, your passion, and your faith.

If you're up to the challenge, it's time to turn the page and get started. The best place to begin, of course, is at the Beginning (with a capital *B*), which, not surprisingly, is **1**.

We can carry the world
on our shoulders,
or we can say,
"I give up, Lord;
here's my life.
I give you my world,
the whole world."

CHAPTER ONE

1-3-12-120-3000

God doesn't want your ability—
He wants your availability.

—

BOBBY BOWDEN

Think for a moment about the difference between wants and needs. When you *want* something (you know that feeling), you have an *urge* to go after it. If you're like most guys, you won't stop until you get it. But needs are very different from wants. You can ignore the things you need for years, for decades, even for a lifetime and scarcely notice what you've been missing.

For example, you need a healthy diet, but you may not want it. You need about eight hours of sleep every night, but you may not get it. You need to focus on your family and your future, but left to your own resources, you may be tempted to focus instead on beer, bad habits, babes, and barbecue.

Life would be much easier if your wants and needs were always the same, but it doesn't work that way. All too often, the things you want you don't need and the things you need you simply don't want.

You'll go through periods when your wants take center stage and your needs are relegated to the nosebleed seats. During these times, your wants can take control of your life, leaving little time and energy for your real needs. So if you haven't been feeling a very big need for God lately, it's possible that your long list of wants may be crowding out your need for God. But the good news is this: the minute you face up to your need for the Father, he responds. God is not hiding or on vacation, so you can always find the Creator *if* you make up your mind to look for him.

Chapter One is the longest chapter in the book for a very good reason. If you don't develop a strong relationship with God, the rest of your life will be more difficult. A relationship with God doesn't guarantee riches and success, but it does guarantee a balanced and fulfilled life. God is wherever you happen to be. He's with you every moment, and he wants to be a full partner in every aspect of your life. That's why the ManCode begins at the very same place your life should begin: *with God*.

Throughout this book we describe your relationship with God as One-to-one. The first *o*, as you might imagine, refers to your Father, while the second *o* refers to you. This construction is intended to remind you that God is God and you're not (even though the world would have you believe it's the other way around). If you're totally committed to a One-to-one relationship with your Creator—if you're wise enough to make God the first page in your life's playbook— you're already destined to be a winner. After all, God has a far better perspective than you. So if you're willing to let the Creator call his plays from the press box (while you refrain from the temptation to call audibles from the line of scrimmage), you'll be victorious.

But if you stubbornly insist on calling your own plays on every snap, you're destined for a losing season. In other words, if you attempt to carve out parts of your life that are separate from God—if you're trying to have a relationship with the Father on Sunday morning while ignoring him the rest of the week—you're setting yourself up for defeat. So remember that God is talking directly to you when he says, "My thoughts are not your thoughts, nor are your ways my ways . . . . For as the heavens are higher than the earth, so are my ways higher than your ways, and my thoughts than your thoughts" (Isaiah 55:8–9, NKJV).

○

God must do everything for us.
Our part is to yield and trust.

—A. W. TOZER

○

The ManCode 1

Bruce Larson, in *Believe and Belong,* tells how he helped people struggling to surrender their lives to Christ: "For many years I worked in New York City and counseled at my office any number of people who were wrestling with this yes-or-no decision. Often I would suggest they walk with me from my office down to the RCA Building on Fifth Avenue. In the entrance of that building is a gigantic statue of Atlas, a beautifully-proportioned man who, with all his muscles straining, is holding the world upon his shoulders. There he is, the most powerfully built man in the world, and he can barely stand up under this burden. "Now that's

COMMANDMENT NUMBER 1 SAYS THAT GOD IS NUMBER 1

The first of the Ten Commandments leaves
no room for interpretation:
"Thou shalt have no other gods before me."
(EXODUS 20:3, KJV)

The story of the Ten Commandments appears twice in the Old Testament, in Exodus 20 and in Deuteronomy 5. When God inscribed his words on those stone tablets, he didn't intend for them to be the Ten Suggestions. Nope, God meant *exactly* what he said. When God gave his ten laws to Moses on Mount Sinai, the Father meant for his commandments to be obeyed with no exceptions, starting with commandment number one, which clearly states that God comes first and everything else comes next.

one way to live," I would point out to my companion, "try-ing to carry the world on your shoulders. But now come across the street with me."

At this point, Larson would take his companions to Saint Patrick's Cathedral on the other side of Fifth Avenue. He would show them another statue, this time of the young boy Jesus. There Jesus is also holding the world, but instead of on his shoulders, it's in his hand. This time there's no burden, no strain; it's effortless. Larson's point is that we get to decide: "We can carry the world on our shoulders, or we can say, 'I give up, Lord; here's my life. I give you my world, the whole world.'"

When Society Wants to Be Number 1

You live in a society that encourages you to relegate God to a few hours on Sunday morning or to ignore him alto-gether. You're part of a culture that encourages you to treat God's laws as mere recommendations, to be accepted or rejected based on your particular circumstances or particu-lar desires. You live in a society that tempts you to think of yourself first, yourself second, yourself third, and God last. That's why it's no surprise that society is so thoroughly confused: society looks to itself for guidance, not to the Creator.

To further complicate matters, you inhabit a world in which a near-infinite number of distractions threaten to gobble up your moments, your days, and your life. Every day you face temptations that are more numerous, more dangerous than ever. You're bombarded with messages that claim you can find (or more accurately "buy") happiness with a woman or at the car lot or in a luxury suite or at the local watering hole. All you've got to do, the world says, is to bet all your chips on the worldly stuff. If you happen to acquire enough man-sized toys, you're set for life. Meanwhile, the world writes God out of the picture.

> If we only believe and ask, a full measure of God's grace is available to any of us.
>
> —CHARLES SWINDOLL

The great irony, of course, is that humanity already possesses everything it needs to acquire genuine peace and abundance. We've already been given clear directions for life here on earth and for life eternal. It's all spelled out in the Bible. But since most guys hate to ask for directions (even when those directions come straight from God), we sometimes refuse to use God's manual. So it's no wonder our lives get messed up. We just can't seem to make ourselves follow the right instructions. The Bible teaches us, "In all your ways acknowledge him, and he shall direct your paths" (Proverbs 3:6, NKJV), but sometimes, in spite of ourselves, we choose the wrong path.

The world's messages are often subtle, encouraging you to do what feels good as long as nobody gets hurt, all the while encouraging you to distance yourself from your Maker. But if you distance yourself from the Creator, somebody *always* gets hurt, and that somebody is always *you*. It doesn't necessarily stop there: other people are injured too. Whenever you detach yourself from God, you'll inevitably—if unintentionally—inflict collateral damage on family members, friends, and even strangers. Yes, ignoring God is dangerous, but this message isn't getting through to large segments of our society.

Society tells you that it's okay to go to church on Sunday—for appearance's sake—but you're not really a man unless you defocus on God and refocus on self and stuff throughout the rest of the week. Too often, we choose to live two lives—one before the "watching world" and another behind closed doors. There, our personal addictions—drinking, computers, fantasy—eat at us, robbing us of our relationships and ultimately defeating us. Only through a personal relationship with Jesus can we find our purpose and the peace that we desire in life. When you establish a One-to-one relationship with God, you learn to live in the world but not worship it. Yet it's tougher than ever to put God first, because the world seems to cry, "Worship me with your time, your money, your energy, and your thoughts!" To resist these temptations, you need a One-to-one focus, a focus that requires genuine obedience, not lip service.

Society has written God out of our public schools and

public places, but you must never write him out of your heart. Are you willing to place God first in your life? Are you willing to welcome God's Son into your heart? Unless you can honestly answer these questions with a resounding "yes," then your relationship with God isn't what it could be or should be. Thankfully, God is always available, and he's waiting to hear from you now. In fact, he's calling to you right now, just like he called out to Adam: "Where art thou?" (Genesis 3:9, KJV). The answer to his calling, of course, is entirely up to you.

Mark it down: things do not "just happen."
There is a God-arranged plan
for this world of ours,
which includes a specific plan for you.

—CHARLES SWINDOLL

Protection against Burnout

When times get tough, during those difficult days when you spend all day working and all night worrying, it's easy to burn out physically, emotionally, and spiritually. But even during the toughest times, you're never alone; your Father is always with you, and you can always turn to him.

The ManCode begins at the very same place your life should begin: with God. If you're totally committed to a One-to-one relationship with your Creator—if you're bound and determined to make God a full-fledged partner in every aspect of your life—you're destined to receive his blessings. But if you try to carve out portions of your life that are apart from God, if you don't connect to Him through respect and obedience, you're setting yourself up for lots of stress and frequent episodes of burnout.

Want an easy-to-use, highly reliable, readily available antidote to stress? It's called prayer, and it means staying in constant, One-on-one contact with your Creator. It means starting each morning with God, talking to him throughout the day, and relying on him at night when you're too worried to sleep.

The stronger your prayer life, the better protection you'll have against the inevitable burdens of twenty-first-century life. So instead of trying to do everything on your own, form the habit of asking God for help. Begin your prayers early in the morning and continue them throughout the day. Remember this: God does indeed answer your prayers in his own way and in his own time. But he's not likely to answer those prayers until you've prayed them.

Daniel Went One-to-one with God

The Bible is full of stories about men who had a One-to-one relationship with God. Daniel was such a man.

Throughout his life, Daniel had sought to align his path with God's plans, so it's not surprising that by the time he was an older man he had worked his way to the top of his profession in the court of King Darius. The king was impressed with Daniel's leadership qualities, so he appointed him to a position of authority in the kingdom. But other men in the palace were jealous, so they plotted to bring Daniel down. Daniel's faith was sorely tested when a couple of his rivals tricked the king into ordering everybody in his kingdom (including Daniel) to worship Darius for thirty days. Daniel, being committed to God, refused, and Darius was forced to toss his trusted adviser into the lions' den.

> God allows us to experience the low points of life in order to teach us lessons that we could learn in no other way.
>
> —C. S. LEWIS

Think for a moment what it must be like to endure an all-night sleepover with a pack of hungry lions. I'm sure Daniel prayed harder than he'd ever prayed in his life, and I'll bet he was more than a little scared. Yet despite the obvious dangers, Daniel had faith because he had already spent a lifetime of getting One-to-one with God. Daniel already knew the power of prayer, so when he was lowered into that pit of ferocious cats, he depended solely on God. It worked!

The next morning, Darius was astounded when Daniel was found alive and well. Soon the king made known his admiration to all:

> Then King Darius wrote to those of every people, nation, and language who live in all the earth: "May your prosperity abound. I issue a decree that in all my royal dominion, people must tremble in fear before the God of Daniel:
> For He is the living God,
> and He endures forever;
> His kingdom will never be destroyed,
> and His dominion has no end.
> He rescues and delivers;
> He performs signs and wonders
> in the heavens and on the earth,
> for He has rescued Daniel
> from the power of the lions."
> So Daniel prospered during the reign of Darius and the reign of Cyrus the Persian.
>
> (DANIEL 6:25–28)

Unlike Daniel, you'll never have to face a den of hungry lions in order to continue practicing your faith, but on some days it may seem like it. The world doesn't take kindly to devoted men who are unwilling to compromise their beliefs.

What forces are asking you to worship the world instead of God? Are certain friends encouraging you to compromise your beliefs? Does your career make worldly demands that would be displeasing to the Creator? Are financial pressures tempting you to violate your values by violating God's laws? If so, you are certainly not alone. Every day you, like all believers, will experience pressures to compromise your faith. Don't give in! Stay One-on-one with God, and he will always stay true to you.

Compromise will rob you of the strength you need to cope with adversity; compromise will deprive you of the abundance that God wants you to experience. Compromise will weaken or even destroy your spiritual foundation. So instead of compromising, be like Daniel: stay true to the living God. When you do, he will strengthen and direct you.

———————————— o ————————————

Man without God is always torn between two urges.
His nature prompts him to do wrong,
and his conscience urges him to do right.
Christ can rid you of that inner conflict.

—BILLY GRAHAM

———————————— o ————————————

Sometimes, You May Find Yourself Wrestling with God

> *The man said, "Let me go; it's daybreak."*
> *Jacob said, "I'm not letting you go 'til you bless me."*
> *The man said, "What's your name?"*
> *He answered, "Jacob."*
> *The man said, "But no longer. Your name is no longer*
> *Jacob. From now on it's Israel (God-Wrestler); you've*
> *wrestled with God and you've come through."*
>
> (GENESIS 32:26–28, MSG)

In Genesis 32 we are told about Jacob's encounter with God. It was quite simply a wrestling match for the ages. Despite exhaustion and weariness, Jacob simply wouldn't let go. Even when God dislocated Jacob's hip, the determined man refused to quit. Even after wrestling all night and after daybreak, Jacob persevered until God finally agreed to bless him. God changed Jacob's name to Israel, which means "he struggles with God." Thus, Jacob formed a spiritual contract as a result of his struggle with—and against—the Creator.

Jacob wrestled with God, and so will you at times. Sometimes you'll struggle to earn God's blessings, and just like Jacob you'll soon discover that the struggle isn't easy. Jacob battled with God before he experienced God's blessing. Perhaps you, too, will grapple long and hard (by trying to do it your way, not God's way) before you finally decide to let God's rules become your rules. The good news is this: when you decide, once and for all, to let God run things, you'll receive the big-time rewards that your Father has in store for you, the kind of rewards that really matter: eternal rewards.

It's worth noting that we human beings find it terribly difficult to view things from an eternal perspective. We want the kind of earthly rewards (fancy cars, big houses, and so forth) that seem, at least to us, to be important. But God sees things differently. He wants us to focus on the important things: the spiritual rewards that last a lifetime. That's what he meant when he said, "Don't collect for yourselves treasures on earth, where moth and rust destroy and where thieves break in and steal. But collect for yourselves treasures in heaven, where neither moth nor rust destroys, and where thieves don't break in and steal. For where your treasure is, there your heart will be also" (Matthew 6:19–21).

So you, like Jacob, should enter into a spiritual contract with your Creator, a rock-steady partnership that binds you to him today, tomorrow, and for a lifetime. As you hammer out the details of that partnership, you'll find that to receive God's blessings you must be obedient to his will. To be obedient to his will, you must try, as best you can, to figure out what he wants you to do with your life. You must follow wherever God leads, even if he leads you through some tough times.

At a meeting of the Fellowship of Christian Athletes, Bobby Richardson, former New York Yankee second baseman, offered a prayer that is a classic in brevity and poignancy: "Dear God, your will, nothing more, nothing less, nothing else. Amen."

—

BOBBY RICHARDSON

God's Got Your Back
(and Front and Sides!)

In Elmer Bendiner's book *The Fall of Fortresses*, he describes a bombing run over the German city of Kassel. Their B-17 sustained heavy fire by Nazi antiaircraft guns. Though heavy fire was expected, what was unusual in this particular instance was that their gas tanks were specifically hit—damage that would normally cause an explosion and likely death. Upon further investigation, Bohn Fawkes, the pilot, discovered that not one but *eleven* unexploded shells were later found in the aircraft's gas tanks.

[Bohn Fawkes] was told that the shells had been sent to the armorers to be defused. The armorers told him that Intelligence had picked them up. They could not say why at the time, but Bohn eventually sought out the answer. Apparently when the armorers opened each of those shells, they found no explosive charge. They were clean as a whistle and just as harmless. Empty? Not all of them.

One contained a carefully rolled piece of paper. On it was a scrawl in Czech. The Intelligence people scoured our base for a man who could read Czech. Eventually, they found one to decipher the note. It set us marveling. Translated, the note read: "This is all we can do for you now."

God Wants You to Be a Winner

Sometimes God allows you to be knocked down by the consequences of your behavior before he lifts you up. He does so, surprisingly enough, because he loves you. He knows that you win when you obey him and you lose when you disobey him, but *you* may not know that. So God may have to let you learn things the hard way, because the easy way simply isn't getting through. Sometimes you must *fall down* before you can be *picked up*. During tough times, it may feel like the Father has given you a whack on the side of the head, when in reality your own choices have caused the pain.

Did you ever have a high school coach who got in your face? If so, you remember that when you made a mistake, Coach got nose-to-nose with you, so close that you could smell the onions he had piled on his lunch. Why did Coach invade your space? The same reason that God needs to. Sometimes you need communication that's simply too clear to misinterpret. Because God has a program that never fails, he wants you to be a contributing member of the winning team.

When we're young, we tend *not* to appreciate the coaches and teachers who make us toe *their* line every step of the way. In fact, we may resent any authority figure who sets clear boundaries and establishes rock-solid expectations. But as we get older, we become more grateful for those rugged disciplinarians who cared enough to make us do our best.

God wants you to do your best, and he knows you can't succeed unless you toe *his* line. So if his discipline seems tough today, rest assured that he has bigger and better things in store for you tomorrow.

———— o ————

What the church needs is not better machinery nor new organizations, but instead it needs men whom the Holy Spirit can use— men of prayer, men mighty in prayer.

—E. M. BOUNDS

———— o ————

The Dominos Guy Delivers More than Pizzas

Tom Monaghan has formed a full-fledged partnership with God, and it's working out quite nicely. But success didn't come easy for the man who practically invented the pizza delivery business. You see, Tom's father died when Tom was only five, and his mother, who was a low-paid domestic worker, tried but failed to hold her family together. So young Tom bounced from one foster home to another until he finally ended up in a Catholic orphanage, where he was forced to focus, at least for a while, on the gospels.

Although the odds were stacked heavily against him— Tom finished dead last in his high school class—Monaghan wasn't a quitter. So with a hard-earned high school diploma in hand, he enlisted in the Marines, served his country, and mustered out with a few dollars, which he promptly invested—and lost—in a worthless oil deal.

There was still a small ray of light at the end of Tom's tunnel, because he and his brother had remained close, and his brother had managed to make a down payment on a tiny pizza shop in Ypsilanti, Michigan. So the two men became partners until Tom's brother found a better job at the local post office. Then, in what may have been one of the best business deals of all time, Tom traded his used Volkswagen Beetle for his brother's half interest in the pizzeria. Now Tom was the sole proprietor of Domino's Pizza.

By now you've probably figured out the rest of the story:

Tom worked hundred-hour weeks, slaved over a hot pizza oven, franchised his pizza restaurants, and made a fortune. To make up for the things he didn't have as a kid, he bought just about everything in sight, including jets, helicopters, mansions, artwork, and even the Detroit Tigers. But none of those things filled the God-shaped hole at the center of Tom's heart. So the alpha-Domino's-guy, remembering the lessons of his youth, finally put things in proper perspective and turned everything back over to God. Tom turned over his heart, his business, his money, and his life—he held nothing back from the Father.

Today, as one of America's biggest contributors to Christian causes, Tom Monaghan is reaching out and making a difference. Yet he's not overly impressed with money. He observed, "I had to get rich to see that being rich isn't important."

What *is* important to Tom—vitally important—is his One-to-one relationship with the Creator.

Can the same be said for you?

———————— o ————————

Jesus Christ is the first and last, author and finisher,
beginning and end, alpha and omega, and by him
all other things hold together. He must be first or nothing.
God never comes next!

—VANCE HAVNER

———————— o ————————

God Has a Plan for You

My (Dennis) dad, Floyd Leon, has always been a man of God, a great father, a devoted husband, and my personal hero. He's shown me how to be a man, and he's shown me what it means to go One-on-one with God. But for the last few years, Floyd Leon has faced a very tough fight because he's been suffering from the gradual, relentless effects of Alzheimer's disease.

Not too long ago, I was visiting my father at a nursing home in Austin, and Dad was, as usual, quite foggy *until* I asked him a question.

"Dad, what's your favorite Bible verse?"

My father's eyes widened and he answered without hesitation: "Proverbs 3:6."

Floyd Leon's quick response reminded me of two important points. First, it showed me that when a good man like my dad spends his whole life in a One-to-one relationship with God, it makes a lasting impression on the man. Even Alzheimer's couldn't rob my father of the memory of his favorite verse.

Second, my father's choice of Proverbs 3:6 showed me how desperately Dad wanted to let God lead the way through every stage of life and beyond. Quoting Proverbs 3:6 was the last thing I heard my father say.

When you establish a genuine, life-altering relationship with God, he will direct your path too. When you put

God first in your life, he'll work in you and through you to achieve his plans and to glorify his kingdom. In fact, the only way to achieve the real purpose for which God created you is to make *him* a full partner in every aspect of your life.

In his best-selling book *The Purpose Driven Life*, Rick Warren reminds us that purpose, like everything else in the universe, begins with God. Whether we realize it or not, God has a plan for each of us, a divine calling, a direction in which he is leading us.

Sometimes God's intentions will be clear to you; at other times God's plan will seem uncertain at best. But even on those difficult days when you are unsure which way to turn, you must never lose sight of these overriding facts: God created you for a reason; he has important work for you to do; he's waiting patiently for you to do it; and he will direct your path if you let him.

The next step is up to you.

> In all your ways acknowledge him, and he shall direct your paths.
>
> –PROVERBS 3:6, NKJV

How God Says "I Love You"

As far back as I can remember, Floyd Leon had a hard time saying, "I love you." Like many fathers of his generation, he was much better at demonstrating love than expressing it verbally. So our conversations often went like this:

ME: "I love you, Dad."

FLOYD LEON: "How are your tires, son. Are you still ridin' on those old maypops? Do you need me to get you a new set of tires?"

ME: "I love you, Dad."

FLOYD LEON: "Your mother talks about you all the time. She wishes you'd write home more. Do you need me to buy you some ballpoint pens? Dennis, here's five bucks; go buy yourself some pens, and try to write your mother a little more often."

ME: "I love you, Dad."

FLOYD LEON: "Dennis, are you taking good care of your feet? When was the last time you bought a decent pair of shoes? Those old things you're wearin' couldn't have any support at all. You know what they say: 'If you take care of your feet, they'll take care of you.' So here's twenty bucks; go get yourself a pair of shoes with some support."

No matter how many times I told my dad that I loved him, he always replied in the same way: by switching the subject and trying to figure out something nice that he could do *for me*. He almost never said "I love you" directly, but he just kept demonstrating his love over and over in many different ways. In the last decade of his life, my dad got better at saying "I love you." I cherish those words, but I also cherish how he showed his love through his life actions.

When you stop to think about it, God says "I love you" in many ways too. Like Floyd Leon, God demonstrates his love time and again by the things he does.

God gives each of us a custom-built package of talents, opportunities, and time here on earth. He showers us with more blessings than we can count, and when we reach the end of our ropes, he gives us the strength to tie a good knot and hang on. When we mess up, he forgives us. When we get lost, he gives us directions. When we skin our knees, he gives us comfort.

God is in the business of dispensing gifts to all humanity, but he reserves his richest blessings for those wise men and women who are willing to establish a One-to-one relationship with him. Will you be a man who puts God first? If you do, then get ready, because the Father will demonstrate his love early, often, and in many different ways . . . just like Floyd Leon.

A FEW MAN-TO-MAN QUESTIONS FOR YOU

1. Tell the truth: Are you really comfortable about your relationship with God? Rate yourself by choosing the sentence below that best describes you. Then put them in the order you think others view you.

   A. You're totally comfortable talking about your faith—or demonstrating it—in just about any situation.

   B. You're comfortable talking about your faith in safe settings (like in church or at home), but you're less likely to express those feelings in less secure settings (like the workplace or at nonchurch public functions).

   C. Even when you're at home or at church, you still find it difficult, but not impossible, to talk about your relationship with God.

   D. You're so uncomfortable with your faith that you never talk to other people about it.

2. List three things that are currently as important (or more important) to you as your relationship with God.

3. Try to visualize what your life might be like if you had a closer relationship with God. Do you think things would be better, worse, or about the same? Be specific. Consider how a closer relationship with the Creator might impact your family, your job, your relationships, or your health.

Before You Move On

At the name of Jesus every knee should bow, of those in heaven, and of those on earth, and of those under the earth, and that every tongue should confess that Jesus Christ is Lord, to the glory of God the Father.

(PHILIPPIANS 2:10–11, NKJV)

The Bible teaches us that Jesus is *the* bridge—not *a* bridge—to God. Period. The Bible makes it clear that at the name of Jesus every knee should bow and every voice should proclaim him as Savior. The Bible instructs us time and again that a real relationship with Christ is *the* unique path not only to earthly abundance but also to eternal life. Nonetheless, in some Christian circles, it has become fashionable to talk *lots* about God and *little* about his Son (meanwhile, the Holy Spirit is often ignored altogether). As strange as it might seem to previous generations of believers—or, for that matter, to the countless martyrs who sacrificed their lives rather than repudiate Jesus—some Christian writers have found it convenient (and popular) to focus on the concept of God while de-emphasizing the other two parts of the Trinity. We don't intend to make that mistake. We believe the Bible means precisely what it says about God, about Jesus, and about the Holy Spirit.

The Holy Spirit

Jesus promised that he would send a Counselor, a Spirit who would reveal God's truth to his followers:

> *And I will ask the Father, and he will give you another Advocate, who will never leave you. He is the Holy Spirit, who leads into all truth. The world cannot receive him, because it isn't looking for him and doesn't recognize him. But you know him, because he lives with you now and later will be in you.*
>
> (JOHN 14:16–17, NLT)

The Holy Spirit should be an important topic for all Christians, but it's a topic that lots of folks ignore. So some of you guys are probably rolling your eyes right about now, thinking that any discussion about the Holy Spirit is either over your head or outside your theology or both. Although millions of words have been written—and almost as many sermons preached—about the miraculous workings of the Holy Spirit, many men still tune out their brains and hearts whenever the subject comes up. In fact, some guys become downright uncomfortable whenever the topic turns to the Spirit with a capital *S*. But Jesus certainly didn't make that mistake. No, the Master wasn't at all bashful about describing the Helper he would send to touch the hearts of his followers and guide their paths. If the Son of God focused on the Holy Spirit, so should we.

Without the Holy Spirit, that Pentecost miracle, as described in the second chapter of Acts, would never have occurred. After all, the Bible teaches us that it was the Holy Spirit who touched the 120 folks who were gathered together on that fateful day (only ten days after Christ's ascension). It was the Holy Spirit who gave those 120 believers the ability to speak in many different tongues, thus launching the tremendous growth of the early church. Here's what happened:

> On the day of Pentecost all the believers were meeting together in one place. Suddenly, there was a sound from heaven like the roaring of a mighty windstorm, and it filled the house where they were siting. Then, what looked like flames or tongues of fire appeared and settled on each of them. And everyone present was filled with the Holy Spirit and began speaking in other languages, as the Holy Spirit gave them this ability.
>
> At that time there were devout Jews from every nation living in Jerusalem. When they heard the loud noise, everyone came running, and they were bewildered to hear their own languages being spoken by the believers.

They were completely amazed. "How can this be?" they exclaimed. "These people are all from Galilee, and yet . . . . we all hear these people speaking in our own languages about the wonderful things God has done!" (ACTS 2:1–11, NLT)

The Holy Spirit transformed the disciples from closed-door believers into lionlike men of boldness. The Spirit energized men to such a degree that Peter (the de-nier) became a bold preacher. The Holy Spirit still works that way. The Holy Spirit has a strengthening effect that allows believers to stop playing defense and start playing offense, and the Holy Spirit offers comfort in times of hard-ship.

When God tugs at your heart, the tug you feel is the Holy Spirit! Are you willing to open your heart and let the Spirit in? If so, you'll be forever changed, and your world will be forever changed too. By welcoming the Spirit into your heart and soul, you'll allow God to work in you and through you. Then, like one of the **120** faithful believers on the day of Pentecost, you'll be destined to change your world and the world.

Remember: the Holy Spirit plays an integral role in the ways that Christians reach out to the world. In Acts 1:8 Jesus proclaimed, "But you will receive power when the Holy Spirit has come on you, and you will be my witnesses in Jerusalem, in all Judea and Samaria, and to the ends of the earth."

The Bible also offers us these insights into the Holy Spirit:

For our gospel did not come to you in word only, but also in power, and in the Holy Spirit and in much assurance, as you know what kind of men we were among you for your sake. (1 THESSALONIANS 1:5, NKJV)

But the Holy Spirit produces this kind of fruit in our lives: love, joy, peace, patience, kindness, goodness, faithfulness, gentleness, and self-control. There is no law against these things! (GALATIANS 5:22–23, NLT)

But when the Helper comes, whom I shall send to you from the Father, the Spirit of truth who proceeds from the Father, he will testify of Me. (JOHN 15:26, NKJV)

Now God has revealed these things to us by the Spirit, for the Spirit searches everything, even the depths of God. (1 CORINTHIANS 2:10)

The Plan of Salvation

So it's time to ask yourself the most important question of all: **Do you have a One-to-one relationship with Jesus?** If you can genuinely answer this question with a resounding "yes," feel free to move ahead to the next chapter. But if you're uncertain or ambiguous about your relationship with Christ, please stop reading now and take time to think about—and more importantly to pray about—your relationship with God and his Son.

Simply put, you need a life-altering, One-to-one relationship with Jesus. Jesus is the way, and there's no side entrance.

Period.

If you don't yet have that relationship, here's how you can get it.

1. Understand that God loves you, and he demonstrated that love by sending his Son in order that you might have abundance and eternal life.

   For God so loved the world, that he gave his only begotten Son, that whosoever believeth in him should not perish, but have everlasting life. (JOHN 3:16, KJV)

   I am come that they might have life, and that they might have it more abundantly. (JOHN 10:10, KJV)

2. Admit that you, like all human beings, have sinned. Sin separates you from God. A spiritual rebirth takes place when you turn your life over to Jesus Christ.

> *For all have sinned and fall short of the glory of God.* (ROMANS 3:23)

> *For the wages of sin is death, but the gift of God is eternal life in Christ Jesus our Lord.* (ROMANS 6:23)

3. Believe that salvation is made possible by Christ's death and resurrection.

> *For Christ also suffered once for sins, the just for the unjust, that he might bring us to God, being put to death in the flesh but made alive by the Spirit.*
> (1 PETER 3:18, NKJV)

> *We have redemption in him through his blood, the forgiveness of our trespasses, according to the riches of his grace that he lavished on us with all wisdom and understanding.* (EPHESIANS 1:7–8)

4. Invite Christ to rule over your heart and your life. When you do, you will be born again.

Therefore repent and turn back, so that your sins may be wiped out. (ACTS 3:19)

For you are saved by grace through faith, and this is not from yourselves; it is God's gift—not from works, so that no one can boast. (EPHESIANS 2:8–9)

5. If you accept what you have just read, pray the following prayer right now:

*Dear Jesus, I am a sinner. But I believe that you died and
rose from the grave so that I might have eternal life.
Come into my heart, Jesus. Take control of my life, forgive my sins,
and save me. I am now placing my trust in you alone
for my salvation, and I accept your gift of eternal life.
Amen.*

What Next?

If you've just prayed the Sinner's Prayer—or if the ideas in this chapter have caused you to rearrange your priorities and your life—it's time to get up out of your chair and do something. Here are three things you can do:

1. Let somebody know what's happened. Call at least one Christian friend and let him know about the changes you've just experienced. In order to strengthen your faith, you need to talk about it. If you don't know another Christian, pray for guidance to reach out to a local pastor. Be watchful, because God will lead you to someone who can help.

2. Make up your mind to become a disciple *today* (because tomorrow may be too late). Jesus doesn't want you to get with the plan someday; he wants you to follow him today:

   Then Jesus said to his disciples, "If anyone wants to come with me, he must deny himself, take up his cross, and follow me. For whoever wants to save his life will lose it, but whoever loses his life because of me will find it." (MATTHEW 16:24–25)

3. Get involved in a church. In order to grow as a Christian, you need to surround yourself with other believers. But you don't have to become a member of the first church you visit. Take time to listen, to pray, to study Scripture, and to ask God to lead you to the right place of worship. He is faithful to lead you to where you should be.

TIME-OUT!

Before moving on to the next chapter, take time to consider these variations of the "God Speaks" billboards, as seen in Cleveland, Ohio:

What part of "Thou Shalt Not . . ."
didn't you understand?

SIGNED, GOD

Keep using my name in vain,
and I'll make rush hour longer.

SIGNED, GOD

Will the road you're on get you to my place?

SIGNED, GOD

(And my personal favorite)

Don't make me come down there.

SIGNED, GOD

God surrounds you
with opportunity.
You and I are free in
Jesus Christ, not to do
whatever we want,
but to be all that God
wants us to be.

—

WARREN WIERSBE

CHAPTER TWO

3

31212 03000

1-3-12-120-3000

*The next best thing to being wise oneself
is to live in a circle of those who are.*

—

C. S. LEWIS

The number 3 stands for your small group, a trio of trustworthy men with whom you can share your thoughts and who will watch your back and hold you accountable. These three guys form your inner circle. They are your most faithful allies and advisers.

The number 3 is negotiable up to a point. You may have two, three, or four guys who make up your team, but if the number gets much larger than that, you'll start spreading yourself too thin (and you might even include someone who won't measure up to the job). So limit yourself to a *few* good men, not many.

These three guys should be men you trust completely. Confidentiality is essential, because you should feel free to talk with these guys about *anything and everything* (remember that confidentiality cuts both ways). Because these men are your most trusted advisers, they should also be fellow believers, strong Christians who don't mind exploring the gospels as they hunker down with you in the foxholes of life. Simply put, you should choose three men who are always available, always loyal, always honest, always faithful, and always willing to help.

Because you're human, you will tend to become more and more like your closest counterparts, not *less* like them. So your inner circle has the power to make you a *better* man (the kind of man God wants you to be) or a *lesser* man (the kind of guy society encourages you to be). And since your 3 will influence you in ways that are both subtle and powerful, you should select guys you really admire.

Can you, without too much hesitation, name at least three men who might fit smoothly into your inner circle? Do you trust these guys—and can they trust you—completely and without hesitation? If so, you and your inner circle are blessed. If not, it's time to start thinking very carefully about the nature, quality, and duration of your closest friendships.

Can You Keep a Secret?

The Duke of Wellington is best remembered as the general who defeated Napoleon at Waterloo in 1815. During his earlier service in India, Wellington was in charge of negotiations after the battle of Assaye. The emissary of an Indian ruler, anxious to know what territories would be ceded to his master, tried in various ways to get the information. Finally, he offered Wellington a large sum of money.

"Can you keep a secret?" asked Wellington.

"Yes, indeed," the man said eagerly.

"So can I," replied Wellington.

—*TODAY IN THE WORD*, JULY 1990, P. 35

Perhaps 3 Is the Most Difficult Number

Most men don't have enough close friends. We guys are excellent at surface friendships, but we're terrible at the other kind. Since we like to pretend we're bulletproof, we don't like to discuss our emotions. After all, if we admitted we had fears or doubts, we'd look weak. Since we believe that real men don't show any weaknesses, we usually avoid talking about our feelings.

As a result, most guys have hundreds of casual acquaintances, plenty of water-cooler colleagues, and enough shoot-the-breeze buddies to last a lifetime. We'll spend thirty minutes holding on a phone line, waiting to spill our guts to a local sports-talk radio host, but when we have the opportunity to have a meaningful conversation with a close friend, we freeze up.

Whether you know it or not, you need a very short list of guys with whom you can talk about *anything*. These are the men who can listen to your fears and learn about your foul-ups without telling *anybody*. These are the few, the strong, the forever friends. They're the trustworthy men who know all about you and love you anyway.

Finding your 3 guys can be tough, especially if you're one of those men who doesn't like to open up. Finding your 3 can be *especially* difficult if you're a man who has difficulty trusting other men. But even if it's tough to create your group of 3, it's worth it.

There's an old adage: When you dig a foxhole, dig it for two. Well, here's the ManCode version: "When you dig a foxhole, dig it for four: yourself and three good men."

When Three Guys Went into the Fire Together

If you'd like to know what can happen when three good men are willing to team up and take the heat *together*, you need look no further than the third chapter of Daniel. There you'll find the story of three men who refused to kneel and worship a statue of King Nebuchadnezzar even though just about everybody else in Babylon had decided to deify their crazy king.

For their trouble, this famous trio—Shadrach, Meshach, and Abednego—were sentenced by Nebuchadnezzar himself to a tortured death inside a blazing furnace. But God had other plans. You see, when these courageous men were tied up and tossed into the flames, they were accompanied—and protected—by a mysterious fourth man who "is like the Son of God."

Shadrach, Meshach, and Abednego weren't casual acquaintances who happened to bump into one another on the way to the execution chamber. No, they were close friends, ready to live together and, if necessary, to die together. They were like three strands woven together into a single rope, stronger together than they could ever be apart.

Can you imagine the conversations those men had

in that fiery furnace? Wouldn't you like to have conversations like that with your closest friends? Well, you'll never experience those kinds of interactions *unless* you're willing to walk into—and through—the fire with them.

So the meaning of the story is clear: when three courageous men banded together for God, they were never alone. God entered the fire with them and shielded them from harm. He'll do the same for your group *if* you let him.

———————————— o ————————————

When you are in the furnace,
your Father keeps his eye on the clock
and his hand on the thermostat.
He knows just how much you can take.

—WARREN WIERSBE

———————————— o ————————————

You Deserve the Experience of Having (and Being) a Confidential Friend

Most men gossip too much. I suppose the same thing could be said about most women, but this book is about guys, so I'll not make any observations about the ladies.

Why are we men tempted to talk too much and too often about other people's business? One reason is that we think it makes us look important when we know things that other folks don't. We think it makes us look like big shots when we're the first man on the block to spill the beans. So whenever we get a juicy tidbit of information, we're tempted to share it with family, friends, neighbors, casual acquaintances, and even strangers. But gossip is corrosive, and it has the potential to hurt both the gossipee and the gossiper. The way that loose talk hurts the person being talked about (the gossipee) is obvious: it exposes some potentially embarrassing fact or an unsubstantiated rumor or maybe even a total falsehood.

The way that gossip hurts the gossiper is less obvious but just as real. For starters, gossip hurts the gossiper because it ruins friendships ("A perverse man sows strife, and a whisperer separates the best of friends"—Proverbs 16:28, NKJV). To make matters worse, gossip is a clear violation of the Golden Rule. Since we don't like being gossiped about, we shouldn't do unto others what we don't want done unto ourselves.

Gossip hurts the gossiper because it is a complete waste of time. Gossip requires energy, inflicts harm on others, and achieves nothing of lasting value.

When a friend shares a private matter with you, that friend deserves your complete confidentiality. You deserve the experience of being the kind of man who can keep his mouth shut. Being a confidential friend is just another way of manning up. You owe it to your friends—and to yourself—to be that kind of man.

Your 3 Can Help You Make Big Decisions

In high school I had the privilege of playing football under those Friday night lights on a team that not only won the Texas 4A state championship but was also named the best high school team in the country.

Upon graduation, I received a full four-year scholarship to Lamar University in Beaumont, Texas. That free ride was a dream come true for me and my parents, but that dream didn't last because, when I arrived at Lamar, things just didn't seem right. Somehow, it seemed that God was calling me in a different direction, and before the school year had even begun, I had decided that Lamar wasn't going to be part of my future. So I said good-bye to Beaumont and headed for home. In fact, I left in such a hurry that I couldn't even contact my parents to let them know I was leaving Lamar.

When I arrived home in Austin, my mom and dad were waiting for me on the front porch. Floyd Leon (one of my 3) made my homecoming easy. Before I had a chance to speak a word, Dad said, "Dennis, your mother and I tried to call you to tell you that if you weren't happy, you should come on back home. But we couldn't get you on the phone. They said you'd already left."

Boy was I relieved! My parents could have raked me over the coals and made me ashamed of my decision. After all, I had just passed up a free four-year education at a great university. But instead of making me feel like a dog, my mom and dad supported me. The very next day another member of my team of **3**, Marshall "Rabbi" Edwards, came to the rescue.

The Rabbi, as we called him, had been my high school chaplain. When he heard the news about my leaving Lamar, he immediately dropped by the house and volunteered to help. The Rabbi, a devout Baptist and a huge fan of Baylor University, loaded my father and me into his car and drove us to Waco. "Dennis," he said, "this is where you're going to go to college." Because of Marshall Edwards' recommendation, they enrolled me at Baylor on a Friday and I was able to start classes the next Tuesday.

My transfer from Lamar to Baylor was made possible by two godly men—men who were concerned not with their own personal gain but with my best interests—who helped me make a decision that changed my life forever. While I was at Baylor, God called me to the ministry, and I've been working for the Lord ever since.

Your 3s Are Your Trash Collectors

Sometimes you just need to get a few things off your chest. You need to gripe, complain, whine, feel sorry for yourself, or express some other form of emotional garbage. Maybe you just need to hear your words spoken out loud.

That's what 3s are for.

Your small group should be comprised of men who can listen to your emotional outpourings, hear about your mistakes, understand your intentions, recognize your faults, and listen to your plans, all without whispering a single word to anybody. You should be able to take your emotional trash to any member of your 3 and leave it with him.

Talking about your problems can help you figure out ways to solve them. Usually, the more you talk, the clearer things become. So you need a few trusted friends who can listen carefully, respond truthfully, and keep your emotional garbage safe for all time.

You'll know that you've found a solid 3 when you're absolutely certain that you can take your innermost problems to any man in your small group without worrying that your words will ever be repeated to anybody.

Your Pastor Can Be One of Your 3s

If you have a close relationship with your pastor, he may certainly become one of your 3s. You can depend upon him for counseling, for advice, for encouragement, for spiritual guidance, for consolation, or all of the above. But just because your pastor is one of your 3s, don't be disappointed if he doesn't ask you to become one of his.

Your pastor undoubtedly ministers to many men and women at your church. He undoubtedly has friends outside the church who depend upon him too. Obviously, it would be impossible for your pastor to include all those people in his own small group. The numbers simply don't work.

So if your pastor becomes a pillar of strength within your 3, thank the Lord for your good fortune. But if you are not a member of your pastor's inner circle, don't take it personally.

Four Words That Every Man Wants to Hear

There are four little words that every man wants to hear: "I've got your back." When you know there are at least three other guys on the planet who have your back, no matter where you are or what you've done, it gives you confidence. When you know that at least three good men are willing to drop whatever they're doing and rescue you from whatever fix you've gotten yourself into, it gives you courage. When you know that you can depend on three good men who will always tell you the truth (even when it hurts) and never gossip behind your back (even to their wives), it gives you the self-assurance to be honest with them *and* with yourself.

Can you name the three guys who've got your back? Can you name three forever friends who are constantly looking out for your best interest, not their own? If you can name them right now, congratulations. But if you're drawing a blank, it's time to start reaching out. It's time to start building your 3.

Five Things to Look for
When Selecting Your **3**

Here are a few of the things you should expect from the men who comprise your inner circle:

1. *Total Honesty:* You should expect unvarnished honesty, no sugarcoating or spin. You can't expect this kind of honest feedback from the people you bump into on the street, but you should expect it from your **3**.

2. *Shared Values:* Select men whose values you admire and whose judgment you trust. These guys aren't perfect, but they'd like to be. Because they're constantly trying to improve themselves, their efforts are bound to rub off on you.

3. *Unwavering Loyalty:* In our no-deposit-no-return world, genuine loyalty is a vanishing commodity. The world may turn against you from time to time, but your inner circle must remain steadfast.

4. *Confidentiality:* Unless you're sure these guys can keep their mouths shut, you'll never be able to confide in them completely.

5. *Staying Power:* Although the men who comprise your group of 3 will probably change as you (and they) enter different phases of life, this group shouldn't be a revolving door. In fact, it's possible that one or two guys will be your inner-circle confidants for life. It's more likely, of course, that you'll have several different inner circles as you grow older, and that's perfectly okay. But if you're trading in best buds faster than you trade cars, it's time to take stock of the way you make—and break—important relationships.

Accountability Is Essential

We live in a world where genuine accountability is the exception and drive-by accountability is the rule. Sure, we're willing to hold ourselves accountable when it's convenient, but we're quick to head for the exits when it's not. Yet there's an obvious problem with here-today-gone-tomorrow accountability: it inevitably leads to seat-of-the-pants decisions that can have dangerous consequences.

Every man is accountable to God, of course. Every man should also be accountable to a few close advisers, a few "willing to get in his face" comrades who aren't afraid to offer friendly-but-frank communication (with a decided emphasis on *frank*). That's the kind of straightforward give-

and-take you should expect from your inner circle. It's a level of honesty you can't expect from casual friends. It's above and beyond the ordinary.

In most relationships, people skim the surface. Sure, they may be honest up to a point, but they're not *too* honest. So what you get is the truth with a little *t*. But with your group of **3** you should expect more; you should expect the unvarnished Truth—truth with a capital *T*. In fact, your three men should form a trio of truth—honest to a fault—because you need at least three guys on the planet who are willing to tell you what you *need* to hear, not what you *want* to hear. Make no mistake: you inhabit a world where honest, constructive criticism is in very short supply.

> Spiritual growth is the process of replacing falsehood with truth.
>
> —RICK WARREN

Perhaps you're one of those guys who can't stand criticism, whether it's constructive or otherwise. Maybe you're a little too fond of trotting out that worn-out litany of excuses every time you feel a little heat. Perhaps you're the sensitive type, a fellow who can't stand the thought of confrontation. If so, get over it. You need honesty far more than you need to feed your own sensitivities.

Being accountable to your group of **3** means that you must forgo any excuse making as you open up and tell your guys what's *actually* going on in your life: the subsurface reality of your world, not the façade you present to every-body else. If you don't open yourself up—or if you start shading the truth to your group of 3—there's no way they can give you meaningful advice, because they don't have all the facts.

Speaking of facts, do you remember the good old days when you, as a student, received detailed evaluations several times a year? Those evaluations were called report cards, and you probably dreaded them like a chicken dreads a fox convention. Well, things have changed plenty since then. Now that you're a grown man, the days of regular report cards are forever gone. Today, you're probably lucky to receive one or two evaluations a year, usually at work, and oftentimes they contain more fluff than substance. So what's a man to do? Well, for starters, you can—and should—depend upon your closest friends to give you honest, excuse-free feedback about your performance as a Christian, as a family man, and as a working man.

Why do you need help evaluating the man in the mirror? After all, shouldn't you be able to grade yourself? Well, not exactly. You're simply too close to that guy in the mirror to be objective, and you're only able to see yourself from one angle. So sometimes you'll be tempted to give yourself straight As when you deserve considerably lower grades. Or you may become your own worst critic, giving yourself failing marks when you deserve better. The truth, of course, is somewhere in the middle. Your inner circle can give you the honest feedback you need to view yourself as realistically as possible.

Good Decisions Are Made in Advance, Not by Impulse

Most of us guys are at least a little impulsive, so we're tempted to make big decisions without taking time to consider the risks. We tend to act first and think second (sometimes, it seems, engaging the brain only as a last resort). When we do, we can get ourselves into big trouble.

If you've ever been victimized by impulsive decision making—or by the impulsive decisions of others—you understand how important it is to look carefully before you leap. But sometimes, one set of eyeballs just isn't enough. That's why you need an accountability group (your inner circle of 3) to help you look things over before the time for leaping arrives.

So here's the one-two-three punch that KOs dumb decisions:

1. Train yourself to pray about everything, even if your prayers are quick, open-eyed conversations with your Father.

2. Rely upon a clear set of principles (before) and take action (after). While you're deciding what

principles to live by, be sure that everything you stand for can be backed up by specific references from God's Word (and while you're reading the Bible, pay close attention to the important insights in the book of Proverbs).

3. If you're about to make a big decision, be sure to talk things over with your 3 guys *before* you make a final decision, not *after*.

When you take these three steps, you'll make solid decisions (not impulsive ones), and you'll avoid needless headaches and heartbreaks.

Close Friends Should Be Willing to Confront Each Other

Sometimes a true friend needs to step into your life and confront you. When that happens, you should be big enough and smart enough to let him into your world and into your thoughts. Why? Because a true friend can sometimes save you from danger, even disgrace, if you let him deal with you nose-to-nose.

It takes a strong man to give someone else access to his life. Are you that kind of man? Can you listen to personal criticism without taking offense, or are you too thin-skinned to hear anything but praise? If you're willing to listen to constructive criticism with an open mind, you'll be doing yourself a big, big favor. But if you're a hard-headed fellow who can't bear criticism, even when it's deserved, you're depriving yourself of valuable information, information that you desperately need. In order to get that information, you need to disclose the whole truth to your closest friends.

As the old saying goes, "Sometimes the greatest untruths are told in silence." In other words, withholding the truth can be, at times, just as harmful as telling a lie. As you think about your communications with your 3, remember this: you should be confident enough to be candid, and you should expect your friends to be equally candid with you.

While it's probably not a good idea to surround yourself with a chorus of full-time critics, you should be willing to listen to the honest appraisals of your closest friends,

---

THE WHOLE TRUTH

You should be confident enough with your 3 to tell the whole truth and nothing but the truth. If you're ever tempted to withhold the truth from a member of your inner circle, slow down for a minute and ask yourself what you're afraid of or what you're hiding from.

---

even when their evaluations are negative. So when a close friend tells you that you're heading down a dead-end street, it's time to think long and hard about turning yourself around before you run headlong into trouble.

Even Jesus Depended on a Few Good Men

Christ had a dozen disciples, but he was closer to some than others. In the gospels we learn that Jesus confided more to—and seems to have had a special relationship with—three disciples: James, John, and Simon Peter.

James is believed by many scholars to be Jesus' first cousin. Because he was bold and energetic, James was called a "son of thunder." He was a dynamic disciple and the first apostle to be glorified through martyrdom. John (also called a "son of thunder") was certainly part of Christ's inner circle (see Matthew 17:1 and 26:37). After Christ's betrayal, it was John and Simon Peter who followed Christ when the others retreated (in fact, it was Jesus himself who changed Simon's name to Peter, which meant, literally, "a mass of the rock." Jesus knew that Peter would be the rock upon which his earthly church would be built).

Shortly before his crucifixion, Jesus went into the Garden of Gethsemane to pray. Who did he take with him? Not surprisingly, it was his three most trusted advisers: James, John, and Peter. It was to John and Peter that Mary first brought the glorious news of Christ's resurrection. So it's no surprise that John and Peter were the first two disciples to go and see the risen Christ.

Yes, even Jesus had an inner circle, a few good men in whom he could confide. If it worked for him, it can work for you too.

Keeping Things in Perspective

Your group of 3 will help you keep things in perspective. In the modern world you're likely to need at least four brains (theirs and yours) to navigate the challenges of everyday life.

For most men, life is busy and complicated. Amid the rush and crush of the daily grind, it is easy to lose focus. When your world seems to be spinning out of control, you must seek to regain perspective by slowing yourself down, talking to your closest confidants, and turning your thoughts toward God.

The familiar words of Psalm 46:10 remind us to "Be still, and know that I am God" (NKJV). The words of Proverbs 27:17 make clear that "as iron sharpens iron, so a friend sharpens a friend" (NLT). Yes, a solid inner circle can help you sharpen your skills and focus your thoughts.

Do yourself a favor: today and every day, be open to God's instruction and be open to your friends' advice. When you do, you can face the day's complications with wisdom, perspective, strength, and hope.

If a temporary loss of perspective has left you worried, exhausted, or both, it's time to readjust your thought patterns. Negative thoughts are habit-forming; thankfully, so are positive thoughts. With practice—and with a little help from your closest comrades—you can form the habit of focusing on God's priorities and your own possibilities.

When you do, you'll soon discover that you will spend less time worrying about your challenges and more time solving them.

───── o ─────

God is bigger than your problems. Whatever worries press upon you today, put them in God's hands and leave them there.

—BILLY GRAHAM

───── o ─────

Have you ever gazed over a string of molehills and imagined that you were looking at the Himalayas? If so, you're not alone. Everybody loses perspective from time to time. But if you make a *habit* of turning molehills into mountains, you'll discover those imaginary peaks will soon become volcanic. So if you've been wasting time and energy fretting about the consequences of some distant possibility, think again. After all, no one ever changed the future by dreading it. Instead of worrying about tomorrow, do today's work and leave the rest up to God. When you do, you'll discover that if you do your part today, the future has a way of taking care of itself.

Things to Look for as Your
Inner Circle Changes over Time

Your Age	Things to Consider as You Choose Your Inner Circle
Approximately Ages 20 to 30	In early adulthood, you're figuring out what it means to be a *real* man as you face up to *real* responsibilities. So look for fellow believers whose values you trust. And while you're at it, look for at least one older man who can give you solid, big-picture advice about your marriage, your career, your future, and your faith.
Approximately Ages 30 to 50	These are years when it's easy to fall for the hollow promises that the world makes but cannot deliver. So look for men who keep you focused on God's values, not the world's values. Find friends who can help you keep your head on straight during these demanding—and at times dangerous—years.
Approximately Ages 50 to 65	For many, these are the most productive years both professionally and personally. As a result, some guys become overly impressed with their own accomplishments. If you're a midlife male who's hitting your stride, find friends who can keep you humble, centered, involved, and (it's worth repeating), humble.
Approximately Ages 65 and Beyond	As the reality of eternity becomes more clearly etched in your brain, look for friends who help you finish strong by staying involved in your faith and your discipleship. You may also look for a few good younger men who need *you* to be *their* mentor.

---------------- o ----------------

A FEW MAN-TO-MAN QUESTIONS FOR YOU ·

---------------- o ----------------

1. Do you have at least three inner-circle friends with whom you can be completely honest? If not, what are you going to do about it? In the space below, name your inner-circle friends:

2. Are you trustworthy? Prove it by going to three close friends and asking them if they'd share something in confidence with you. Then record your results by selecting the sentence (A, B, or C below) that best describes the answers you receive:

A. All three friends indicate you're completely trustworthy. They'd tell you just about anything. These responses show that you're a reliable, mature, non-gossipy guy. Congratulations.

B. At least one of your friends indicates he might be hesitant to share a big secret with you. This response means that you probably still have a thing or two to learn about confidentiality.

C. Two or three of the guys you talk to express reservations about sharing confidential information with you. This means you've still got some growing up to do. The best day to begin growing up is today.

3. Pick the sentence below (A, B, or C) that best describes you:

A. You're willing to listen to—and learn from—close friends when they hold you accountable for your actions.

B. When your closest friends call you to account, you may not like what you hear—and you may not take their advice—but you're not hostile.

C. You simply cannot stand the idea of other people telling you what to do, so you don't welcome—and you do not usually accept—advice from anybody, even your closest friends.

What Next?

Now that you've seen the need for a three-man inner circle, what are you going to do about it? Here are several things you can and should do:

1. If you're not yet the kind of man whom your closest friends can trust completely, it's time to grow up. Remember that your inner circle of 3 will never be effective until you find the courage and the wisdom to be totally trustworthy.

2. Talk to God about the three guys who should make up your inner circle. If you're not certain who your 3 guys are, take the next three weeks and pray about your decision. If God only reveals one or two men to you, start there and wait for God to help you fill out your small group at a time of his choosing.

3. Now that you've settled on the names of the men who you would like to comprise your small group. Pray for them and approach them individually to discuss their being a part of your inner circle. Make sure that your discussions are face-to-face, not over the phone.

TIME-OUT!

Before moving on to the next chapter, let's take a break from the heavy stuff and enjoy this bit of comic relief:

This Friday, we invite you to attend our FASTING & PRAYER Conference. The cost for attending the Fasting and Prayer conference includes meals.

The peacemaking meeting scheduled Wednesday night has been canceled due to a conflict.

At the evening service tonight, the sermon topic will be "What Is Hell?" Come early and listen to our choir practice.

Ladies, please don't forget the rummage sale next Saturday. It's a chance to get rid of those things not worth keeping around the house. Don't forget your husbands.

This afternoon there will be a meeting in the south and north ends of the church. Children will be baptized at both ends.

Weight Watchers will meet at 7 p.m. in the Fellowship Hall. Please use the large double door at the side entrance.

Thursday night will be a potluck supper. Prayer and medication to follow.

A wise leader chooses
a variety of gifted
individuals.
He complements
his strengths.

—

CHARLES STANLEY

CHAPTER THREE

12

31212 03000

1-3-12-120-3000

*Fortify yourself with a flock of friends!
You can write to one, dine with one,
visit one, or take your problems to one.
There is always at least one who will
understand, inspire, and give you the lift
you may need at the time.*

—

GEORGE MATTHEW ADAMS

The third number in the ManCode is **12**, a number that signifies a broader circle of good friends—men you can do things with, men you can share good times with, men who can help you get things done. Of course Jesus enlisted a dozen disciples who came from varied backgrounds. You need at least a dozen men who, while certainly not as close as your inner circle of **3**, comprise a personal network of go-to guys.

The first two numbers in the ManCode are straightforward: the number **1** signifies your relationship with God, and it's nonnegotiable. The number **3** signifies a clearly identified accountability team composed of Christian men who will help you plan for the future and who will hold you accountable for your actions. But your group of **12** may not be quite so easy to identify, because these men may have differing perspectives and differing backgrounds.

Will some of the men in your **12** be from your church? Probably, but not all of them should be. You need more variety than that.

Will all the members of your **12** ever gather in one place? Probably not. In fact, unless you're living in a very small town, some of the men in your **12** may not even know one another.

Should all the men in this expanded circle be Christians? Probably not, and that's good, because it gives you opportunities to reach out and share your faith with good friends. What is certain is this: each man in your **12** should make a positive contribution to your life. That means that each man in your **12** should be a source of *positive* peer pressure—a constructive influence in a decidedly negative world.

As you think about the guys who will comprise this larger circle of friends, look for men who:

1. You enjoy being with
2. Are available
3. Are boosters, not cynics
4. Exert a positive influence on your life

Don't be concerned if you can easily name more than a dozen guys who might fit into your **12**. On the other hand, if you've wracked your brain and you can't name twelve good men, it's time to start expanding your reach.

At Least One Member of Your 3 May Also Be in Your 12

Can you have crossover friends who do double duty in both your **3** and your **12**? Of course you can. But it's probably a good idea to have at least one member of your inner **3** who is clearly *outside* the social landscape of your **12**. Why? Because you need at least one key adviser who can help you engage in outside-the-box thinking, and that probably means you need at least one man who isn't completely immersed in the everyday realities of your world.

Your **3** won't change much over time, but this is not true for your **12**. While you shouldn't consider your **12** to be a revolving-door group of quick-changing acquaintances, neither should you expect the group to be permanent. After all, because you're dealing with the lives and careers of *at least* a dozen men, you should expect—and even welcome—a certain amount of change within the group.

By the way, if you're heavily involved in your community, you may have several groups of **12**. You might, for example, be a member of a tight-knit men's Bible study group *and* an active participant in a local service club *and* a booster at your kid's school *and* a contributing member of the local business community, *and* the list goes on.

Can a Non-Christian Be in Your Group of *12*?

It's ironic that some guys, especially those who take their faith seriously, seem hesitant to establish meaningful friendships with non-Christians. The irony, of course, stems from the fact that Christ himself created a ministry that reached out to *everybody*. Jesus didn't isolate himself in the relative safety of a few like-minded believers. Far from it. Christ extended himself to Jews and Gentiles, to rich and poor, to sinners and saints. If it was good enough for him, it's good enough for you.

One of the great experiences for a Christian man is to lead another man to Christ. But guess what? If you never have a meaningful conversation with a nonbeliever, you're unlikely to lead *anybody* to Jesus.

So don't hesitate to establish friendships outside the church. You are the light, and you're only here on earth for a short visit. While you're here, you should shine as brightly—and as widely—as you can.

Men Need to Spend Time with Other Men

Whoever said, "It's a man's world," wasn't living in the twenty-first century. Today, the differences between the sexes are seldom celebrated and often minimized. Whether it's in the workplace or at a local health club or just about anyplace in between, men and women are tossed in together, usually with far too little time for guy-to-guy interaction.

In the good old days, if you went to the local YMCA to work out, you entered an all-guy world, a place where you could be yourself. But today, if you're down at the Y sweating off a few pounds on the treadmill, you may be surrounded by women, with scarcely another man in sight. It's no longer a man's world. For better or for worse, it's a coed world, pure and simple. But just because the world doesn't see the value of guys hanging out with guys doesn't mean that you should go along with the idea. You need good men—and more than a few of them—to hang out with, to talk with, to learn from, to have fun with, and to accomplish things with.

While you're with your **12,** you shouldn't constantly feel compelled to give sermons, to lecture, to preach, or to teach theology. The best way to show another guy that you're a Christian is to behave like one. When you do the simple things—like counting every stroke on the golf course or refusing to take a second look at a woman in a short skirt—you may disclose more about your faith than if you had delivered a year's worth of sermons. So think of your **12,** not as a flock that needs to be preached to, but as a group of guys who can help you enjoy the game of life while you're improving your skills. Even if you're very good at what you do, your skills can still be sharpened. And your **12** can help.

———— o ————

God has a plan for your friendships because He knows your friends determine the quality and direction of your life.

—CHARLES STANLEY

———— o ————

Sharpening Your Ax

When you surround yourself with about a dozen good friends, you'll be shaped and sharpened by a few good men.

> A young man approached the foreman of a logging crew and asked for a job.
> "That depends," replied the foreman. "Let's see you fell this tree." The young man stepped forward and skillfully felled a great tree.

Impressed, the foreman exclaimed, "You can start Monday."

Monday, Tuesday, Wednesday, Thursday rolled by—and Thursday afternoon the foreman approached the young man and said, "You can pick up your paycheck on the way out today."

Startled, the young man replied, "I thought you paid on Friday."

"Normally we do," said the foreman. "But we're letting you go today because you've fallen behind. Our daily felling charts show that you've dropped from first place on Monday to last place today."

"But I'm a hard worker," the young man objected. "I arrive first, leave last, and even have worked through my coffee breaks!"

The foreman, sensing the young man's integrity, thought for a minute and then asked, "Have you been sharpening your ax?"

The young man replied, "No sir, I've been working too hard to take time for that!"

Our lives are like that. We sometimes get so busy that we don't take time to sharpen our ax. In today's world, it seems that everyone is busier than ever but less happy than ever. Why is that? Could it be that we have forgotten how to stay sharp?

Who Packs Your Chute?

Charles Plumb was a US Navy jet pilot in Vietnam. After seventy-five combat missions, his plane was destroyed by a surface-to-air missile. Plumb ejected and parachuted into enemy hands. He was captured and spent six years in a communist Vietnamese prison. He survived the ordeal and now lectures on lessons learned from that experience.

One day, when Plumb and his wife were sitting in a restaurant, a man at another table came up and said, "You're Plumb! You flew jet fighters in Vietnam from the aircraft carrier *Kitty Hawk*. You were shot down!"

"How in the world did you know that?" asked Plumb.

"I packed your parachute," the man replied. Plumb gasped in surprise and gratitude. The man pumped his hand and said, "I guess it worked!"

Plumb assured him, "It sure did. If your chute hadn't worked, I wouldn't be here today."

Plumb couldn't sleep that night, thinking about that man. Plumb says, "I kept wondering what he might have looked like in a Navy uniform: a white hat, a bib in the back, and bell-bottom trousers. I wonder how many times I might have seen him and not even said 'Good morning, how are you?' or anything because, you see, I was a fighter pilot and he was just a sailor." Plumb thought of the many hours the sailor had spent on a long wooden table in the bowels of the ship, carefully weaving the shrouds and folding the silks of each chute, holding in his hands each time the fate of someone he didn't know.

Now, Plumb asks his audience, "Who's packing your parachute? Everyone has someone who provides what they need to make it through the day." Plumb also points out that he needed many kinds of parachutes when his plane was shot down over enemy territory—he needed his physical parachute, his mental parachute, his emotional parachute, and his spiritual parachute. He called on all these supports before reaching safety.

Sometimes in the daily challenges that life gives us, we miss what is really important. We may fail to say hello, please, or thank you, congratulate someone on something wonderful that has happened to them, give a compliment, or just do something nice for no reason.

—AUTHOR UNKNOWN

Betrayal Is a Possibility

Jesus chose Judas in his **12**, knowing that in the fullness of time Judas would betray him. Even Peter, in a moment of weakness, denied Christ.

You, like the Master, may experience betrayal within your group of **12**. So don't expect that every man in the group will be perfectly loyal or trustworthy. In fact, don't be surprised if a member of this group sells you out. But if you're betrayed, remember that the disloyalty, as painful as it may be, is still part of God's plan for your life. Could it be that the lesson in the betrayal is more important than the fun and the friendship? Probably so.

Sometimes, you must accept the fact that occasional betrayals are part of God's grand design—and his grace is always available to the betrayer. After all, Peter became the rock of the church *after* he denied Christ.

———————————— o ————————————

God has a plan for the life of every Christian. Every circumstance, every turn of destiny, all things work together for your good and for his glory.

—BILLY GRAHAM

———————————— o ————————————

Go Tell

The Living Bible translates 1 Corinthians 9:22, "whatever a person is like, I try to find common ground with him so that he will let me tell him about Christ and let Christ save him." Randy Raysbrook of the Navigators in the January–February 1994 issue of *Discipleship Journal* gives some pointers in finding that common ground:

- Be natural. Normal conversation is fluid and respectful, allows for humor, and invites response.

- Be open and willing to admit your struggles and failures.

- Be respectful, look at people for what they are as well as what they can become.

- Be simple. Communication increases as simplicity does. Don't let Christian jargon get in the way.

- Don't forget what it was like to be a non-Christian.

- Look forward to hindsight. Unbelievers will understand some things only after looking back on them.

—*LIFELINE* (A MEN'S LIFE EVANGELISM NEWSLETTER), FALL 1995

○

A FEW MAN-TO-MAN QUESTIONS FOR YOU

○

1. Can you name a dozen men with whom you can form a strong circle of friends—men you can spend time with, have fun with, and learn from? If so, list those men below.

2. Now that you've listed at least a dozen men, list each guy again and give him a grade on a sliding scale from 1 to 10, with 10 meaning that he has a totally positive impact on your life and 1 meaning that he has become a negative influence. After you've graded each man on your list, consider carefully what the list says about

the nature, quality, and the future direction of your friendships. While you're at it, don't be impatient with the imperfections of your friends, just as you hope they won't be impatient with yours.

As you think about the men you've described on the previous page, remember that God cares for every person on that list and so should you. So don't ostracize a friend just because you've given him a low rating. Instead of giving up on him, try a different approach. Try leading him to Christ.

3. Rate yourself as a member of the **12**. If all your friends were like you, would your friendships be stronger, weaker, or nonexistent?

TIME-OUT!

It's time to take another break: enjoy!

Caution: Church driver of this vehicle
subject to fits of praise!

Give Satan an inch and he'll be a ruler.

Today is a gift from God.
That's why it is called "The Present."

Forbidden fruits create many jams.

The Rapture . . . separation of church and state!

In case of nuclear attack . . .
the ban on school prayer is lifted.

Try this home improvement: take your family to church.

The wages of sin is death—quit before payday!

I work for a Jewish Carpenter.

No Jesus, no peace. Know Jesus, know peace!

Heavenly forecast: Jesus will REIGN forever!

Cars aren't the only thing recalled by their maker.

In our faith we follow in someone's steps.
In our faith we leave footprints to guide others.
It's the principle of discipleship.

—

MAX LUCADO

CHAPTER FOUR

120

31212 03000

1-3-12-120-3000

The Bible knows nothing
of solitary religion.

—

JOHN WESLEY

The fourth number in the ManCode is **120**—a number that stands for the local church. In the second chapter of Acts, shortly after Christ ascended into heaven, **120** of his disciples were touched by the Holy Spirit. This small but powerful group of men became the foundation of the early church, so we've chosen the number **120** to represent Christ's church. Make no mistake: you and I *are* the church. When we come into a relationship with Jesus, we, like believers of every generation, become like Peter, of whom Christ said, "Upon this rock I will build my church" (Matthew 16:18, KJV). So please don't think of the church as merely a freestanding collection of bricks and mortar, because it's more than that. Much more!

Far too many folks go to church for the wrong reasons: to get something from other members or to put an imaginary checkmark on some self-imposed cosmic to-do list or to fulfill a family tradition or simply out of habit. But none of these reasons is good enough. Why, then, should you get out of bed (or off the golf course) to worship God in his church? It's simple:

You should go to church to grow and to give.

If your church allows you to continue growing in your faith—and if you've found a place where you can enthusiastically give of your talents, your treasure, and your time— you're worshiping at the right place. But if you're simply taking up space in a pew for an hour or two on Sunday mornings—and if you're not totally sure why you're sitting there—it's time to rethink your priorities, your place of worship, and your participation. While you're thinking, remember that if you have a problem with the church, the problem probably has as much (or more) to do with *you* than with the church you're attending.

You won't *get* much out of any church unless you're willing to *give* something to that church (and the something we're talking about here is not necessarily money). If you ever stop giving to the church, you'll soon become disgruntled. So the only way you'll *really* be satisfied in a church is to be a contributing member of your church. There's really no other way. What happens if you become burned out on church? The answer is to become *more* involved, not *less*.

Don't get too hung up on the physical structure where worship takes place. Can church happen in a basement in China? Of course it can. Does it happen at the biggest megachurch on the planet? Certainly. Can it happen anyplace in between? Absolutely. God says, "Where two or three are gathered together in my name, I am there among them" (Matthew 18:20). So the size of your church, its name brand, or its physical characteristics aren't nearly as important as the size of the things you experience there.

Church is a place to fill yourself and give yourself away. It's a place where you become a part of something much bigger than yourself. It's a place where two plus two may equal five or five thousand or five million. This kind of supernatural multiplication occurs *through* the church because God chooses to bless the efforts *of* his church. Whether it's a mission trip to a foreign land, disaster relief after a hurricane, or using five loaves and two fish to feed thousands, God always partners with his church to bless their efforts.

Give Your Kids That Old-Time Religion

Not so long ago, before the advent of the modern media, back in the days when youngsters still performed manual labor and lots of it, young folks flocked to church because it was one of the few places where they could be with other kids. After working six hard days (often in the fields), youngsters viewed church as a welcome change of pace. So they didn't dread church; they embraced it.

> The church is not an end in itself; it is a means to the end of the kingdom of God.
>
> —E. STANLEY JONES

Yes, in the good old days the church was not only the center of family life but also the center of community life. Not so anymore. In today's world, popular culture seems to have taken the place of the church as the foundation of societal values, and we're worse off because of it. So it's no wonder that our young people are struggling to find their way in a world that honors materialism and instant gratification, not morality.

Common sense tells us—and the Bible teaches us—that it's important to introduce our youngsters to the church at an early age. So if you're a dedicated dad who wants what's best for your kids (and if you're a dedicated dad, you do), you'll make certain that your youngsters are in church and that you're right there with them.

So here are some timely questions. What are you going to do to make church as attractive to your children as it was to your grandparents when they were kids? Are you going to give up or give more: more to your family, more to the church, more to God?

You Need the Church More than the Church Needs You

Perhaps you've been under the misconception that the church needs you. Well, not exactly. You see, you need the church *far more* than the church needs you. This certainly doesn't mean that the church won't benefit from your help, and it doesn't mean that you shouldn't be a contributing member to your local fellowship. What it does mean is this: if you're doing things right, you'll *always* get more out of a church than you put into it.

God doesn't need for you to attend church. *You* need the experience of attending, as Hebrews 10:24–25 explains,

"Let's see how inventive we can be in encouraging love and helping out, not avoiding worshiping together as some do but spurring each other on" (MSG). God doesn't need your money; *you* need the experience of giving it to him. God doesn't need your time or your talents—he already has infinite quantities of those—but *you* need the experience of sharing. God clearly can accomplish his work without your assistance, but he desires to work through you so you can be blessed in the process.

You need the fellowship and the gifts you can find in the local church. You need the variety of people you find there: people with different personalities, professions, and attitudes; people who will be there for you and your family when you need them. Without the church, you are like a single burning coal that's separated from the fire; you'll lose energy and heat. You don't want that to happen. That's why fellowship with other believers should be an integral part of your everyday life.

You also need to witness the supernatural multiplication that can happen when a church *really* gets serious about changing the world. You need to see firsthand the marvelous things that God can do when cooperative Christians reach out to the needy. You need to be an eyewitness and an active participant in the mission field. You need to see how congregations can transform the lives of people around the corner or around the globe. You need to witness these things as part of a team, not as a soloist.

Jesus understood networking. When he wanted to share his message, he called upon his church to help do it. Nothing has changed since then. Today, God wants the world to see his church in action. That's why Christians are often the first and most effective responders to natural disasters (such as Hurricane Sandy). It's why so many churches help form the backbone of organizations like Habitat for Humanity.

> Only participation in the full life of a local church builds spiritual muscle.
>
> —RICK WARREN

Whether your church has 120 or 1,200 or 12,000 souls, it is meant to be a powerful tool for spreading God's good news and uplifting his people. God intends for you to be a fully contributing member of the church. If you know what's good for you, your intentions will be the same.

Men with Backbone Should Be the Backbone of the Church

If you visit any church, it's easy to gauge the health of that church by looking at the folks who are sitting in the pews. If there are plenty of fully grown, church-loving, Bible-believing, fellowship-building men present and accounted for, the church is in good shape. But if you see many more women than men, you should ask yourself, "Where have all the guys gone? Are they all down at the bowling alley or at the lake fishing or on the golf course or out at the softball diamond? Why have they abandoned their church?"

That isn't to say, of course, that God doesn't call women to contribute mightily to his church—of course he does. But in far too many congregations, it seems that women are being asked to do most of the heavy lifting. Why? Because when it comes to the vital business of building the local church, far too many men have gone AWOL—they are missing in action.

Men need to be actively involved in the church because we were made for the church. It's our natural home. That's why we should *never* sit back and let the women do most of the work and most of the worship. Instead, we must stand up and be counted. We need to see more fathers worshiping with children, more husbands worshiping with wives, and more men taking leadership roles in the church. We need men to provide strength and stability in the church. We need more men's classes, more men's groups, and more men's ministries. Yes, we need them badly, and we need them *now*.

It's true that many churches don't seem to be man-friendly. It's almost as if they were catering to a feminine demographic. While much more could be written on this subject, suffice it to say that the local church is ministering to the people who are coming through their doors, and most of those folks, at least in recent years, are women. This trend is quite a change from the days of old.

In Old Testament times, women weren't even *allowed* inside certain parts of the temple. But we're living in New Testament times, which means we worship together—men side by side with women—and thank goodness we do. Yet too many fully grown guys are missing that opportunity, the opportunity of worshiping alongside their wives and children. Make sure you're not one of them.

Uncle Sam Isn't the Only One Who Needs You

Every American is familiar with Uncle Sam, the star-spangled personification of national patriotism. In fact, if you close your eyes, you can probably see Sam clad in red, white, and blue, pointing his finger squarely (and seriously) in your direction as he says, "I want you!"

Well, Uncle Sam isn't the only one who needs your help. Your pastor needs it too. Why? Because your pastor is doing the most important work of all: the work of sharing the message of God's Son. Of course all the numbers of the ManCode are directly related to Jesus, our shepherd. But the number **120** addresses the special relationship that you should have with God's under shepherd: your pastor.

Jesus Himself was surrounded and supported by men. We men, in turn, must surround and support our pastors, because they're our leaders, the shepherds who protect our particular flocks. We must honor each pastor's calling and

REAL MEN DO

- The typical US congregation draws an adult crowd that's 61% female, 39% male. This gender gap shows up in all age categories.
- On any given Sunday there are 13 million more adult women than men in America's churches.
- This Sunday almost 25% of married, churchgoing women will worship without their husbands.
- Over 70% of the boys who are being raised in church will abandon it during their teens and twenties. Many of these boys will never return as men.
- More than 90% of American men believe in God, and five out of six call themselves Christians. But only two out of six attend church on a given Sunday. The average man accepts the reality of Jesus Christ but fails to see any value in going to church.

These trends continue each year, painting a dismal picture for men in the church. (churchformen.com) recognize his role in God's kingdom. Being a pastor is a demanding seven-day-a-week job, a job with more pressures than most of us realize. Sometimes pastoring a church can be a lonely endeavor. So you can be sure that your minister, like Uncle Sam, needs as many good men as he can muster.

Your pastor needs men to help build the church and serve its members. He needs honest, clear-thinking friends to advise him, and he needs trustworthy men to watch his back when times get tough. Your pastor needs men to help him find other men, new members who can help grow the church by pitching in and rolling up their sleeves for the Lord. In short, your pastor needs men like you, men who are ready, willing, and able to serve.

———— o ————

The church is where it's at. The first place of Christian service for any Christian is in a local church.

—JERRY CLOWER

———— o ————

Your pastor is worthy of his hire. He answers to the Lord, and he must someday give an accounting of his work. A man with such demands and responsibilities needs genuine counsel, courtesy, compassion, and encouragement. He needs more than a few good men. In fact, he needs a church full of men who, by working together, can become an army of One.

Perhaps you can be an inner-circle **3** to your pastor. Or maybe you will become a member of his **12**. In any event, you should always strive to be a contributing member of his **120**. No exceptions!

So if you take no other idea from this book, please remember these three words: Support your pastor. He deserves your help, and you deserve the experience of giving it to him.

Protect Your Pastor and Speak Up for Him

As a pastor-in-training, I needed all the help and every single bit of sound advice I could get. One of my mentors, Herschel Hobbs, gave me a helpful hint about the best way to handle church meetings. He said, "Dennis, as a pastor, you can't just say the first thing that comes into your head. When something needs to be said, the first thing you should do is to wait. If you keep quiet, one of the good men in the church will usually say what needs to be said."

He was right. I soon discovered that when something needed to be said in a church meeting, the most courageous men in my pastorate would inevitably speak up.

Your pastor needs *you* to stand up for him and to speak up for him whenever two or more members of your church are gathered. There are some things that your pastor might like to say but can't. Whenever he cannot speak up for himself, for whatever reason, you should take it upon yourself to speak for him.

Floyd Leon's Big Question

A few years after my father began exhibiting the signs of Alzheimer's disease, we all decided it was time for Floyd Leon to stop managing the household money. So we talked to our accountant and then had a lawyer draw up the papers. When time came for Dad to sign on the dotted line, we found ourselves seated around a conference table with our family members, our accountant, our lawyer, and my father.

As the lawyer slid the papers in front of Floyd Leon, I spoke up: "Dad, do you have any questions?"

"Just one," he replied.

All of us held our breath. Was Floyd Leon going to ask some off-the-wall question? Or, heaven forbid, was he going to change his mind?

After a moment of silence, I said, "We've got all the time in the world, Dad. What do you want to know?"

"I've just got one question," my father replied as his eyes began to mist. "Can I still write out my tithe check?"

We were all stunned. Here we were, talking to a fellow who was about to sign over the control of his entire net worth, every penny he had ever saved during a lifetime of hard work, and his only question concerned the 10 percent he put in the offering plate every Sunday.

Floyd Leon was serious about his tithe.

Are you that serious about *yours*?

Don't Look for Perfection at Your Church

Even without knowing the name of your church, I can tell you something about it: it's not perfect.

No church is perfect, because every church is comprised of imperfect people. In fact, every church gets a little dysfunctional at times because its members are a little dysfunctional at times too.

So if you're looking for the perfect church, prepare to be disappointed. Perfect churches, like perfect congregations, simply don't exist.

Ten (Mythical) Reasons Not to Go to Church with (Real) Responses in Parentheses

Reason 1: Everybody in church is a hypocrite.
(No, *everybody* in church *isn't* a hypocrite, and your own negativity doesn't make it a reality.)

Reason 2: The church doesn't meet my needs.
(Lots of people in the church are trying hard to meet your needs. Are you looking past these folks or for them?)

Reason 3: Church takes up too much time. (Sure church takes time. But so does watching the

Golf Channel, the NFL, NASCAR, and
American Idol. Which is more important?)

Reason 4: They're always asking for money. (No,
they're not *always* asking for money. Besides, if
every guy gave what he should give, the church
wouldn't need to ask for money.)

Reason 5: I don't like the preacher. (The preacher
is trying to get through to you. How hard are
you trying to let him get through?)

Reason 6: I had a bad experience in the church.
(No place is perfect. You've had bad experiences
everywhere: at work, at home, at school, and
just about every place in between. But you
probably didn't quit work or drop out of school
at the first sign of trouble, and if you did give
up, the common denominator is you.)

Reason 7: The music is too loud. (Really?)

Reason 8: The music isn't loud enough. (If so,
why are you still sitting in the last pew?)

Reason 9: The Sunday school classes are boring.
(Your church obviously needs a few more good

teachers. By the way, when was the last time you taught?)

Reason 10: Someone sat in my pew last week.
(Your pew? Maybe the trespasser thought it was God's pew.)

A FEW MAN-TO-MAN QUESTIONS FOR YOU

1. Besides giving money, can you list at least three other ways you've contributed to the life of your church during the last six months? Write them below.

2. If everybody else in your church contributed as much as you do, would your church be stronger, weaker, about the same, or out of business?

3. How creative can you be in thinking of ways to contribute to the life of your church? Below, list at least five new ideas for service, five things you can do during the coming year to strengthen your church.

What Next?

1. If you're not involved in a local church, the most important thing on your to-do list is to find one that fits you and your family. Below jot down some of the things you would like in a church. Spend time in prayer over the next several days and ask God to direct you. Be proactive. Starting this Sunday, visit churches in your area.

2. Can you point to three ways you've grown as a result of attending church?

3. If you're already a member of a church, take an inventory of your participation on the lines below. Are you really active or are you just taking up space? Be brutally honest with yourself. Make note of specific things you can do to give more to your church and to grow more in your faith.

TIME-OUT!

It's time to have a few laughs together!
Here are some of my favorite church signs:

FOR MEMBERS ONLY.
Trespassers will be baptized.

Redemption Center—No Coupons Needed

If you're looking for a sign from God
to get back to church, this is it!

This is just a little country church
with a lost and found.

This Church is on fire!
But you don't need to call 911.

GODISNOWHERE (now read it again)

Come in and let us prepare you for your finals.

Free trip to Heaven! Details inside!

Our faith grows
by expression.
If we want to keep
our faith,
we must share it.

–

BILLY GRAHAM

CHAPTER FIVE

3000

31212 03000

1-3-12-120-3000

*Jesus calls us not only to come to him,
but to go for him.*

—

RICK WARREN

The ManCode ends where it began: by taking a careful look at your relationship with God. The first number of the ManCode deals directly with your One-to-one relationship with the Creator. The final number in the ManCode, the number **3000**, deals directly with your response to God's calling, a mission he has placed in your heart, your calling to serve others.

Think for a moment about the early church in the days immediately after Christ's ascension into heaven: the eleven disciples along with Matthias (the man who replaced Judas so the disciples might once again form a complete group of **12**) gathered with **120** new Christians, all crowded into the Upper Room, that sacred place where the last supper had been served less than two months before. Many of these men had just spent forty days with the risen Christ, but now Jesus was gone.

On that same day the **120** gathered in the Upper Room, Peter spoke to a large group in Jerusalem, and **3000** men and women were baptized. This occurred on the day that was the Jewish feast of Pentecost, a day that was a defining moment in the early church.

So the number **3000** stands for *reach* and *service*: your need to reach out to the world by translating God's good news into your own good deeds.

Jesus had clear instructions for all his disciples: "Go into all the world and preach the gospel to the whole creation" (Mark 16:15). But Jesus wasn't implying that all of us should become preachers. He knew from experience that most guys wouldn't stand up in front of a crowd and give a sermon. No, Jesus wanted us to preach his gospel, not just with our mouths, but with our hands and feet. That's what the number **3000** is about: serving God by going out in the world and serving others.

The Tug

Have you ever felt God tugging on your heart? Have you ever had the feeling that God wanted you to go somewhere or do something for him? Have you ever felt the need to give more, to sacrifice more, or to do more for God by doing more for his children, whether those people were on the other side of town or the other side of the globe? The honest answer to each of these questions (whether you realize it or not) is yes.

Every day of your life, God is tugging you in a particular direction, the direction he wants you to go. But if you're like most of us hardheaded men, you may be resisting that tug. After all, you already have your own strategy and your own to-do list (not to mention your own wish list). If you're like most males, you secretly want to be a take-charge kind of guy, a rugged individualist who charts his own course, picks

> If it doesn't affect your hands and feet, it isn't Christianity.
>
> —JESS MOODY

his own fights, solves his own problems, feeds his own ap-
petites, and makes his own plans. But the trouble begins
when *your* plans don't bear any resemblance to *God's* plans.
When that happens, something's got to give.

Some men spend entire lifetimes resisting God's tug.
Like lounge singers doing a poor Frank Sinatra imitation,
they insist upon doing things "My Way" instead of *his* way.
By resisting God's call, they miss out on the best life has to
offer.

Other men—and we sincerely hope you'll include
yourself in this number—finally respond to God's tug.
They realize the tug they feel comes from the Creator of
the universe, and they respond accordingly. They ask God
for guidance, they listen for his responses, they step beyond their comfort zones, and they begin doing big things
for him. These men are the real heroes of God's kingdom.
These are the men who lead the families, who build the
churches, who serve the local communities, and who reach
out to the world. These are the dads, the coaches, the
boosters, the counselors, the rehab faciliators, the mentors,
the Big Brothers, the chaplains, the Sunday school teachers, and the scoutmasters who help make the world better
one kid at a time. These are the guys who are willing to get
involved—and stay involved—in the life of their church,
in the lives of their friends, and in the lives of people they
don't even know. These are the men who are *really* re-
sponding to Christ's great commission. They're taking the

gospel to the world, and they're preaching it—sometimes with words but more often with work. They're doing things *with* God and *for* God. When they do, they've successfully dialed in the ManCode's final number.

God's tug is not a push. He will not force you to do something against your will. But what he will do is this: he will stand at the door of your heart and invite you to help others. He will lead you to people who need your help, and he will invite you to help them. He certainly won't compel you to help, but he'll encourage you to help. The rest is up to you.

How can you be absolutely certain that the tugs you feel are from God? Simple: God's tug always leads you to do something for others, not for yourself. The tug, if it is from God, is not about getting more things for you. It's never about more money, more possessions, more fame, more pleasure, or more gratification. No, God's tug isn't about getting; it's about giving. Giving more of yourself to others.

But there's a paradox: by giving things away, you always receive more in return than you give. It's simply another form of spiritual multiplication. That's why the Bible says, "It is more blessed to give than to receive" (Acts 20:35, NKJV).

When you answer God's tug, you've formed a partnership with the Creator of the universe. The time to form that partnership is now.

Manning Up for the Multiplied Life

When you man up for God, your efforts are multiplied—and that's no accident. God's Word promises time and again that when we give him what little we have, he will take our humble offerings and do great things with them.

We guys like to be on the winning team. Whether we're playing on the field or cheering from the sidelines, we like the feeling of victory and we detest defeat. We want to be part of something big, something exciting, something that gives purpose and meaning to our lives.

After his resurrection, Jesus addressed his disciples:

But the eleven disciples proceeded to Galilee, to the mountain which Jesus had designated. When they saw him, they worshiped him; but some were doubtful. And Jesus came up and spoke to them, saying, "All authority has been given to me in heaven and on earth. Go therefore and make disciples of all the nations, baptizing them in the name of the Father and the Son and the Holy Spirit, teaching them to observe all that I commanded you; and lo, I am with you always, even to the end of the age."

(MATTHEW 28:16–20, NASB)

Christ's great commission applies to men of every generation, including this one. As believers, we are called to share the good news of Jesus Christ with our families, our neighbors, and the world. Yet many of us are slow to obey the last commandment of the risen Christ; we simply don't do our best to "make disciples of all the nations." Although our personal testimonies are vitally important, we are often hesitant to share our experiences. That's unfortunate.

Billy Graham observed, "Our faith grows by expression. If we want to keep our faith, we must share it." If you are a follower of Christ, the time to express your belief in him is now.

You know how Jesus has touched your heart; help him do the same for others. You must do likewise, and you must do so today. Tomorrow may indeed be too late.

———————————— o ————————————

Our Lord is searching for people who will make
a difference. Christians dare not dissolve into
the background or blend into the neutral
scenery of the world.

—CHARLES SWINDOLL

———————————— o ————————————

Discipleship Now

Jesus' disciples came from all walks of life: blue-collar and professionals, including fishermen and a tax collector. They were from different political spectrums, including some passionate revolutionaries. These men came with diverse personalities and emotional traits, from Peter the impulsive to Thomas the doubter.

God is still in the business of acquiring disciples: ditchdiggers and presidents; Republicans, Democrats, and Independents; introverts and extroverts. His only criteria are that you *believe* in him and that you be willing to *live* for him.

God has blessed you with unique opportunities to serve, and he has given you every tool you need to do so. Today, accept this challenge: value the talent that God has given you, nourish it, make it grow, and share it with the world. After all, the best way to say thank-you for God's gifts is to use them.

God wants you to stay sharp in his work, and you can do so by using the ManCode as your guide. So keep God as your number-one priority, stay close to your friends, be an active participant in your church, and keep reaching out to the world. Remember that the ManCode is an ongoing work. It's like when you go to the gym: you unlock your locker every day. Unlocking your potential is an everyday activity, and your combination is

1 3 12 120 3000

How to Share the ManCode

In his second letter to Timothy, Paul speaks to believers of every generation when he writes, "God has not given us a spirit of timidity" (1:7, NASB). Paul's meaning is clear: when sharing our testimonies, we must be courageous, forthright, and unashamed.

When we let other people know the details of our faith, we assume an important responsibility: the responsibility of making certain that our words are reinforced by our actions. When we share our testimonies, we must also be willing to serve as positive role models, undeniable examples of the changes that Jesus makes in the lives of those who accept him as their personal Savior.

So here's a word of caution: don't share the ManCode with others unless you're willing to live the ManCode. Why? Because the things you say about your faith are not nearly as important as the way you live your faith.

Genuine faith, the kind of faith that moves hearts and mountains, is better demonstrated than announced. In other words, it's perfectly fine to tell people about your beliefs, but it's far more effective to show them the results of your beliefs. The good news is this: when you live your faith day in and day out, in good times and hard times, other men notice. After all, most of us guys are more interested in results than theories. We may listen to the things other people say, but we watch even more carefully what other people do. We are, by and large, like the good folks from Missouri, the Show Me State. We like things we can see up close and personal. Then we make judgments for ourselves.

When we can see with our own two eyes that the ManCode is working for another guy, we're more likely to buy into the program. If not, we're likely to walk away sooner rather than later. So if you make the ManCode your personal code, remember it's never enough to talk about the ManCode; you also should make up your mind to become a living, breathing example of the ManCode in action.

─────────── o ───────────

A FEW MAN-TO-MAN QUESTIONS FOR YOU

─────────── o ───────────

1. Now that you're up to speed on all of the ManCode numbers, do you honestly believe that this Code can work for you? Answer yes or no: _____

2. If you answered no to question 1, what sort of personal code are you living by today? What code do you intend to live by tomorrow?

3. If you answered yes to question 1 above, give yourself a letter grade (A, B, C, D, F) that represents your assessment of how you're currently addressing each number in the ManCode:

Your relationship to 1: _____

Your relationship to 3: _____

Your relationship to 12: _____

Your relationship to 120: _____

Your relationship to 3000: _____

If you just gave yourself straight As, perhaps it's time for some honest self-evaluation (unless, of course, you're a modern-day saint, which you probably aren't).

What if your grades were less than spectacular? If so, don't beat yourself up. Focus on the areas that need improvement, and start doing whatever it takes to improve your grades.

What Next?

Now that you've graded yourself, it's time to let a few other folks grade you too. Ask three or four people—and if you're married, ask your wife—to give you a letter grade (A, B, C, D, F) for each number in the ManCode. Ask each person to offer candid assessments. Discourage flattery and encourage honesty. Jot down their evaluations in the spaces below.

	1	3	12	120	3000
1. _____					
2. _____					
3. _____					
4. _____					

Were you surprised by anybody's assessment? What do your friends' and family's grades, combined with your own, have to say about the condition of your spiritual health? What areas of the ManCode need immediate attention?

TIME-OUT!

Sunday School Stories

Nine-year-old Joey was asked by his mother what he had learned in Sunday school.

"Well, Mom," he said, "our teacher told us how God sent Moses behind enemy lines on a rescue mission to lead the Israelites out of Egypt. When he got to the Red Sea, he had his army build a pontoon bridge and all the people walked across safely. Then, he radioed headquarters for reinforcements. They sent bombers to blow up the bridge and all the Israelites were saved."

"Now, Joey," asked the mother, "is that *really* what your teacher taught you?"

"Well, no," he replied. "But if I told it the way the teacher did, you'd never believe it!"

———— o ————

A Sunday school teacher asked, "Johnny, do you think Noah did a lot of fishing when he was on the ark?"

"No," replied Johnny. "How could he, with only two worms?"

Let us not be content
to wait and see what
will happen, but give us
the determination to make
the right things happen.

—

PETER MARSHALL

CHAPTER SIX

SO NOW WHAT?

1-3-12-120-3000

*Then one of the criminals who were
hanged blasphemed him, saying,
"If You are the Christ, save yourself and us."
But the other, answering, rebuked him,
saying, "Do you not even fear God,
seeing you are under the same
condemnation? And we indeed justly,
for we receive the due reward of our deeds;
but this man has done nothing wrong."
Then he said to Jesus, "Lord, remember me
when you come into your kingdom."*

—

LUKE 23:39–42, NKJV

Three wooden crosses stood on the hill that day. Soldiers gathered nearby, gambling to see who would win Christ's garments. Two of the condemned men were thieves who certainly deserved some sort of punishment, but the third figure, the One who claimed to be the Son of God, was blameless.

While hanging on his cross, one thief taunted Jesus; the other thief asked him for mercy. One thief chose to blaspheme the Son of God while the other chose to worship him. So the wise thief ended his life that day, but he did not perish. After breathing his last, that man awoke in the arms of the eternal One, his Savior.

We know very little about the thief who accepted Christ. We have no details about his life, whether he ever experienced a 3 or a 12 or a 120. But what we do know is this: that man reached out in his last moments here on earth and became a powerful example to the world by achieving the final number of the ManCode: the 3000. His story has touched the hearts of millions and will continue to echo throughout eternity.

Choices. You must make hundreds of them every day, thousands every week, hundreds of thousands every year. But only one choice will determine your destiny on earth and throughout eternity. That choice, simply stated, is this: what will you decide to do about Jesus?

You are free to choose, as one of the thieves did, to say no to Christ. You can choose to mock the Son of God in an overt fashion or you can choose a more subtle form of mockery by professing to be a Christian with your words but not with your actions. In either event, you'll rob yourself of the abundance and joy that might otherwise be yours in him. Or you can make a different choice.

If you choose to say yes to Jesus—completely and without reservation—you'll experience a personal and spiritual transformation. You'll become a different man, a different husband, a different father, a better servant to the world. When you say yes to Christ, you receive his love and companionship today, tomorrow, and forever. It's a blessing beyond belief and beyond compare.

The choice is yours and yours alone.

The ManCode Is a Self-Diagnostic Tool

If you're experiencing tough times, you can use the Man-Code to perform a quick but effective way to understand your problems. Here's how to make the diagnosis:

1. First, ask yourself if you have the 1 in your life.
2. Next: Do you have a strong 3 and (just as important) are you using them?
3. Next: Are you surrounded by an active, involved 12?
4. Are you a positive, faithful, contributing member of an enthusiastic 120?

5. Are you tapping into your **3000** by reaching out to your community and to your world? Are you finding meaningful ways to serve God and share his good news?

If you've attended to the five numbers of the Man-Code, you'll begin to achieve a sense of balance in your life. But if these numbers are not right—if you lack even a single number in the ManCode—you'll need to make things right before you can expect to receive the best things that God has planned for you.

So put all your numbers in place and get ready for God to do some important work in and through you.

———————————— o ————————————

God's various gifts are handed out everywhere; but they all originate in God's Spirit. God's various ministries are carried out everywhere; but they all originate in God's Spirit. God's various expressions of power are in action everywhere; but God himself is behind it all. Each person is given something to do that shows who God is: Everyone gets in on it, everyone benefits. All kinds of things are handed out by the Spirit, and to all kinds of people!

–1 CORINTHIANS 12:4–7, MSG

———————————— o ————————————

Personal Bible Study and Proverbial Wisdom

Every man needs the benefit of regular Bible study, so make sure your 3—and at least some members of your 12—are encouraging you to stay focused on regularly studying God's Word.

———— o ————

A wise man will listen and increase his learning, and a discerning man will obtain guidance.

–PROVERBS 1:5

———— o ————

When your troubles threaten to make you feel like a living, breathing tackling dummy (and everybody plays the dummy from time to time), the answers you need are as close as the nearest Bible. God's Word doesn't grow old, and it doesn't go out of style. It contains timely, practical instructions for every aspect of your life. When in doubt, consult your Bible. A great place to start is the book of Proverbs.

Proverbs contains 31 chapters. So when you read a chapter a day, you can easily finish the whole book in a month. When the next month rolls around, you can turn back to chapter 1 and restart the whole process.

When you make Proverbs a regular part of your daily Bible study, you'll weave God's wisdom into the fabric of your day. You'll start tackling life's problems *before* they tackle you.

CodeKillers

To implement your own personal ManCode, you must learn to defeat a dangerous collection of vices we call CodeKillers. CodeKillers are the destructive behaviors, the mistaken attitudes, the bad habits, and the chronically misdirected thought patterns that create distance between you and God. Just about any bad habit you can name has the power to come between you and the Lord, and when it does, warning bells should start going off in your brain.

We can all think of men who were destroyed by their own addictions, whether drugs, alcohol, women, or gambling. We've all known guys whose inability to grow up and behave like real men caused untold suffering for themselves and their families. Of course, it goes without saying (but we'll say it anyway) that you certainly don't want to find yourself caught up in personal self-destruction like that.

So here's a Ten Most Wanted List of CodeKillers that you should watch for and run from. These CodeKillers can wreck your life and, in some cases, even end it. Be on the alert for these self-destructive tendencies and do whatever it takes to vanquish them. Or else!

1. *Addiction*: If we become addicted to any substance or behavior, the addiction begins to rule our lives. The addiction comes first, ahead of God or just about anything else, for

that matter. Whenever we relegate God to a secondary position in our hearts and minds, we always suffer.

2. *Dishonesty*: God is truth and he loves truth. Whenever we are dishonest, whether with others or with ourselves, we create a wall—a needless and destructive wall—between ourselves and our Creator.

3. *Bitterness*: Bitterness focuses on the unfairness of the past. But God intends for us to focus on his unimaginable gifts and on the blessings he has in store for us. When we become embittered, we focus too intently on yesterday, and we fail to thank God for his blessings and his love *today*.

4. *Greed*: When we focus too much on acquiring money or possessions, the things we're striving to obtain become substitute gods. They inevitably separate us from the One true God.

5. *Hopelessness*: When we abandon hope, we're saying (at least on an unconscious level) that our problems are simply too big for God. Our failure to trust him leads, not surprisingly, to

even more helplessness. It's a very dangerous cycle.

6. *Impulsiveness*: Throughout the Bible, God instructs us to think first and act second (if you don't believe it, try reading a few chapters in Proverbs). So when we *act* first and *think* second, we're disobeying God (and inviting unwelcome consequences as a result).

7. *Irrational Fear*: Some fears are rational, and some fears are not. The irrational kind causes us to become stuck in emotional quicksand. While we're stuck, we cannot become the men God wants us to be.

8. *Immaturity*: Some of us never quite seem to grow up, and in some respects that's good. After all, it's healthy to retain a childlike sense of wonder and excitement. But not all forms of immaturity are healthy, and when men shirk their responsibilities while behaving like irresponsible schoolboys, God isn't pleased and eventually he shows it.

9. *Chronic Anger*: Some men seem to stay angry most of the time. It's a shame because all that

anger leaves little or no room in their hearts for joy, love, praise, or thanksgiving.

10. *Apathy*: Some men seem to give up on life and, without realizing it, on God. Once they've given up, it can be very hard for these fellows to jump-start their lives. But the good news is this: with God, all things are possible, including life-altering, soul-transforming jump starts for apathetic men.

CodeKillers are always destructive, but they are *never* insurmountable. In fact, the minute you decide to overcome any personal shortcoming, God stands ready to help you succeed. With him, all things are possible. If you sincerely ask for his help in the struggle against CodeKillers, he will give it. So ask him. Now.

Life is a series of choices between
the bad, the good, and the best.
Everything depends on how we choose.

–VANCE HAVNER

The ManCode Personal Inventory

The following pages contain several examples of a brief, easy-to-understand, self-administered questionnaire that you can use to gauge your own progress in each of the five ManCode categories.

After you've read the examples in this section, please take a minute to fill in the first blank questionnaire. Be as honest with yourself as possible and, after you've rated yourself for each ManCode number (1–3–12–120–3000), jot down the implications of your scores on the lines provided beneath the five rankings.

Over time, your circumstances will change and so might your survey scores. So, in a month or two, fill in a second questionnaire, date it, and compare it with your first one. Then, once each quarter—or whenever you feel the need—revisit these pages and take a few minutes to rate yourself again.

Each time you take this inventory, you'll be able to assess your present situation and compare it with past scores. In this way, you can judge the direction of your spiritual journey as it relates to your Creator, to your friends, to your church, and to the world.

Things to Think About as You Assess Your Scores

1: Rating Your Relationship with God

This score is the foundation upon which every other aspect of your life is built. If you establish a rock-solid relationship with God, he can guide you through, and beyond, the darkest days of life. But if your spiritual relationship is weak, or almost non-existent, then you'll constantly be at risk in every other area of your life.

3: Assessing the Relationship with Your Small Group

These men hold you accountable, and they help keep your life in balance. If you have a loyal group of men whom you can call upon at any time for support and advice — and if you do, indeed, call upon them often — you're less likely to lose direction or lose perspective. But, a low score in this area means that you may be vulnerable to irrational thinking or to impulsive behavior, or both.

12: Your Broader Circle of Good Friends

If you grade yourself with a lower score in this area, you may be feeling isolated and vulnerable to the inevitable changes that are a part of modern life. And a low score may mean that you're missing out on opportunities for friendship, learning, and fun. A higher score in this category means that you're reaching out to your buddies in positive ways, and that's a good thing for you and for them.

120: Assessing Your Involvement at Church

In this category, give yourself the highest score if you're a fully contributing, regularly attending, non-complaining member of your congregation. A low score means that you may be vulnerable to negativity or cynicism as it relates to church. As you think about your score, don't forget that your involvement in church is inextricably related to your relationship with the Creator: a stronger participation in your local church will help you build a stronger relationship with the Lord.

3000: Rating Your Reach and Your Service

If you're actively reaching out to your community and to the world, give yourself a high score in this category. A lower score means it's probably time to start praying about your priorities.

SAMPLE SCORES AND PROFILES

EXAMPLE #1:

ManCode Number	Poor	Marginal	Good	Rock Solid
1: Quality of your current relationship with God	1	2	3	(4)
3: Quality of your current relationships with the members of your small group	(1)	2	3	4
12: Quality of your current relationships with your **12**	1	(2)	3	4
120: Your contribution at church	1	2	(3)	4
3000: Your contribution to your community	1	2	(3)	4

Profile: loves God but struggles with relationships. If this applies to you, you are in need of accountability and friends ASAP! Make these needs a matter of prayer.

EXAMPLE #2:

ManCode Number	Poor	Marginal	Good	Rock Solid
1: Quality of your current relationship with God	✓ 1	2	3	4
3: Quality of your current relationships with the members of your small group	1	✓ 2	3	4
12: Quality of your current relationships with your **12**	✓ 1	2	3	4
120: Your contribution at church	✓ 1	2	3	4
3000: Your contribution to your community	✓ 1	2	3	4

Profile: no relationship with God and very little account-ability to his small group; quite likely unhappy or even miserable; may have difficulties maintaining a healthy mar-riage; gives little of himself to others or to charity.

EXAMPLE #3:

ManCode Number	Poor	Marginal	Good	Rock Solid
1: Quality of your current relationship with God	**X**	2	3	4
3: Quality of your current relationships with the members of your small group	**X**	2	3	4
12: Quality of your current relationships with your 12	1	**X**	3	4
120: Your contribution at church	1	2	**X**	4
3000: Your contribution to your community	1	2	**X**	4

Profile: active in church, but distant from God; little accountability to mentors or peers; keeps up appearances, but is secretly unsure of himself; sometimes experiences major lapses in judgment.

EXAMPLE #4:

ManCode Number	Poor	Marginal	Good	Rock Solid
1: Quality of your current relationship with God	1	2	3	4
3: Quality of your current relationships with the members of your small group	1	2	3	4
12: Quality of your current relationships with your **12**	1	2	3	4
120: Your contribution at church	1	2	3	4
3000: Your contribution to your community	1	2	3	4

Profile: a confident man who is focused and friendly; is accountable to his small group of close friends and mentors; has a definite sense of purpose; knows where he's going; is willing to make changes when necessary; recognizes the value of others.

MANCODE QUESTIONNAIRE
WHERE AM I?

Name: _____

Date: _____

Rate Yourself from 1 to 4 with 4 being the highest.

ManCode Number	Poor	Marginal	Good	Rock Solid
1: Quality of your current relationship with God	1	2	3	4
3: Quality of your current relationships with the members of your small group	1	2	3	4
12: Quality of your current relationships with your **12**	1	2	3	4
120: Your contribution at church	1	2	3	4
3000: Your contribution to your community	1	2	3	4

Implications of Your Rankings:

Specific Ways to Improve:

MANCODE QUESTIONNAIRE
WHERE AM I?

Name: _____

Date: _____

Rate Yourself from 1 to 4 with 4 being the highest.

ManCode Number	Poor	Marginal	Good	Rock Solid
1: Quality of your current relationship with God	1	2	3	4
3: Quality of your current relationships with the members of your small group	1	2	3	4
12: Quality of your current relationships with your **12**	1	2	3	4
120: Your contribution at church	1	2	3	4
3000: Your contribution to your community	1	2	3	4

Implications of Your Rankings:

Specific Ways to Improve:

MANCODE QUESTIONNAIRE
WHERE AM I?

Name: _____

Date: _____

Rate Yourself from 1 to 4 with 4 being the highest.

ManCode Number	Poor	Marginal	Good	Rock Solid
1: Quality of your current relationship with God	1	2	3	4
3: Quality of your current relationships with the members of your small group	1	2	3	4
12: Quality of your current relationships with your **12**	1	2	3	4
120: Your contribution at church	1	2	3	4
3000: Your contribution to your community	1	2	3	4

Implications of Your Rankings:

Specific Ways to Improve:

MANCODE QUESTIONNAIRE
WHERE AM I?

Name: _____

Date: _____

Rate Yourself from 1 to 4 with 4 being the highest.

ManCode Number	Poor	Marginal	Good	Rock Solid
1: Quality of your current relationship with God	1	2	3	4
3: Quality of your current relationships with the members of your small group	1	2	3	4
12: Quality of your current relationships with your **12**	1	2	3	4
120: Your contribution at church	1	2	3	4
3000: Your contribution to your community	1	2	3	4

Implications of Your Rankings:

Specific Ways to Improve:

MANCODE QUESTIONNAIRE
WHERE AM I?

Name: _____

Date: _____

Rate Yourself from 1 to 4 with 4 being the highest.

ManCode Number	Poor	Marginal	Good	Rock Solid
1: Quality of your current relationship with God	1	2	3	4
3: Quality of your current relationships with the members of your small group	1	2	3	4
12: Quality of your current relationships with your 12	1	2	3	4
120: Your contribution at church	1	2	3	4
3000: Your contribution to your community	1	2	3	4

Implications of Your Rankings:

Specific Ways to Improve:

MANCODE QUESTIONNAIRE
WHERE AM I?

Name: _____

Date: _____

Rate Yourself from 1 to 4 with 4 being the highest.

ManCode Number	Poor	Marginal	Good	Rock Solid
1: Quality of your current relationship with God	1	2	3	4
3: Quality of your current relationships with the members of your small group	1	2	3	4
12: Quality of your current relationships with your 12	1	2	3	4
120: Your contribution at church	1	2	3	4
3000: Your contribution to your community	1	2	3	4

Implications of Your Rankings:

Specific Ways to Improve:

MANCODE QUESTIONNAIRE
WHERE AM I?

Name: _____

Date: _____

Rate Yourself from 1 to 4 with 4 being the highest.

ManCode Number	Poor	Marginal	Good	Rock Solid
1: Quality of your current relationship with God	1	2	3	4
3: Quality of your current relationships with the members of your small group	1	2	3	4
12: Quality of your current relationships with your 12	1	2	3	4
120: Your contribution at church	1	2	3	4
3000: Your contribution to your community	1	2	3	4

Implications of Your Rankings:

Specific Ways to Improve:

MANCODE QUESTIONNAIRE
WHERE AM I?

Name: _____

Date: _____

Rate Yourself from 1 to 4 with 4 being the highest.

ManCode Number	Poor	Marginal	Good	Rock Solid
1: Quality of your current relationship with God	1	2	3	4
3: Quality of your current relationships with the members of your small group	1	2	3	4
12: Quality of your current relationships with your **12**	1	2	3	4
120: Your contribution at church	1	2	3	4
3000: Your contribution to your community	1	2	3	4

Implications of Your Rankings:

Specific Ways to Improve:

MANCODE QUESTIONNAIRE
WHERE AM I?

Name: _____

Date: _____

Rate Yourself from 1 to 4 with 4 being the highest.

ManCode Number	Poor	Marginal	Good	Rock Solid
1: Quality of your current relationship with God	1	2	3	4
3: Quality of your current relationships with the members of your small group	1	2	3	4
12: Quality of your current relationships with your 12	1	2	3	4
120: Your contribution at church	1	2	3	4
3000: Your contribution to your community	1	2	3	4

Implications of Your Rankings:

Specific Ways to Improve:

MANCODE QUESTIONNAIRE
WHERE AM I?

Name: _____

Date: _____

Rate Yourself from 1 to 4 with 4 being the highest.

ManCode Number	Poor	Marginal	Good	Rock Solid
1: Quality of your current relationship with God	1	2	3	4
3: Quality of your current relationships with the members of your small group	1	2	3	4
12: Quality of your current relationships with your **12**	1	2	3	4
120: Your contribution at church	1	2	3	4
3000: Your contribution to your community	1	2	3	4

Implications of Your Rankings:

Specific Ways to Improve:

MANCODE QUESTIONNAIRE
WHERE AM I?

Name: _____

Date: _____

Rate Yourself from 1 to 4 with 4 being the highest.

ManCode Number	Poor	Marginal	Good	Rock Solid
1: Quality of your current relationship with God	1	2	3	4
3: Quality of your current relationships with the members of your small group	1	2	3	4
12: Quality of your current relationships with your **12**	1	2	3	4
120: Your contribution at church	1	2	3	4
3000: Your contribution to your community	1	2	3	4

Implications of Your Rankings:

Specific Ways to Improve:

MANCODE QUESTIONNAIRE
WHERE AM I?

Name: _____

Date: _____

Rate Yourself from 1 to 4 with 4 being the highest.

ManCode Number	Poor	Marginal	Good	Rock Solid
1: Quality of your current relationship with God	1	2	3	4
3: Quality of your current relationships with the members of your small group	1	2	3	4
12: Quality of your current relationships with your **12**	1	2	3	4
120: Your contribution at church	1	2	3	4
3000: Your contribution to your community	1	2	3	4

Implications of Your Rankings:

Specific Ways to Improve:

APPENDIX

We'll wrap things up with a collection of timely, practical, thought-provoking quotations from noted Christian men. By the way, if you haven't already done so, you should probably start jotting down favorite quotations in a place where you can review them often.

ABOUT WISDOM

Knowledge is horizontal.
Wisdom is vertical; it comes down from above.
—BILLY GRAHAM

The fruit of wisdom is Christlikeness, peace,
humility, and love. And, the root of it is faith
in Christ as the manifested wisdom of God.
—J. I. PACKER

The more wisdom enters our hearts,
the more we will be able to trust our hearts
in difficult situations.
—JOHN ELDREDGE

The man who prays ceases to be a fool.
—OSWALD CHAMBERS

If you lack knowledge, go to school.
If you lack wisdom, get on your knees.
—VANCE HAVNER

ABOUT THE IMPORTANCE OF MAKING GOOD DECISIONS

Every time you make a choice, you are turning
the central part of you, the part that chooses, into
something a little different from what it was before.

—C. S. LEWIS

Good and evil both increase at compound interest.
That is why the little decisions you and I make every day
are of such infinite importance.

—C. S. LEWIS

Every day, I find countless opportunities to decide
whether I will obey God and demonstrate my love
for him or try to please myself or the world system.
God is waiting for my choices.

—BILL BRIGHT

Life is a series of choices between the bad, the good,
and the best. Everything depends on how we choose.

—VANCE HAVNER

Successful people make right decisions early
and manage those decisions daily.

—JOHN MAXWELL

ABOUT NOT GIVING UP

God sometimes permits us to experience humiliating
defeats in order to test our faith and to reveal
to us what's really going on in our hearts.

—WARREN WIERSBE

You've got problems; I've got problems;
all God's children have got problems.
The question is how are you going to deal with them?

—JOHN MAXWELL

Life will be made or broken at the place
where we meet and deal with obstacles.

—E. STANLEY JONES

When you fall and skin your knees and skin your heart,
he'll pick you up.

—CHARLES STANLEY

Only the man who follows the command of
Jesus single-mindedly and unresistingly
lets his yoke rest upon him, finds his burden easy,
and under its gentle pressure receives the power
to persevere in the right way.

—DIETRICH BONHOEFFER

ABOUT FAMILY

The first essential for a happy home is love.

—BILLY GRAHAM

A family is a place where principles are hammered and
honed on the anvil of everyday living.

—CHARLES SWINDOLL

The only true source of meaning in life is found
in love for God and his son Jesus Christ,
and love for mankind, beginning with our own families.

—JAMES DOBSON

Every Christian family ought to be, as it were,
a little church, consecrated to Christ,
and wholly influenced and governed by his rules.

—JONATHAN EDWARDS

The family circle is the supreme conductor
of Christianity.

—HENRY DRUMMOND

ABOUT LEADERSHIP

When God wants to accomplish something,
he calls dedicated men and women to challenge
his people and lead the way.

—WARREN WIERSBE

People who inspire others are those who see
invisible bridges at the end of dead-end streets.

—CHARLES SWINDOLL

The great illusion of leadership is to think that
others can be led out of the desert by someone
who has never been there.

—HENRI NOUWEN

You can never separate a leader's actions
from his character.

—JOHN MAXWELL

Nothing speaks louder or more powerfully
than a life of integrity.

—CHARLES SWINDOLL

ABOUT THE NEED TO SERVE

You can judge how far you have risen in the scale
of life by asking one question: How wisely and how deeply
do I care? To be Christianized is to be sensitized.
Christians are people who care.

—E. STANLEY JONES

In Jesus, the service of God and the service
of the least of the brethren were one.

—DIETRICH BONHOEFFER

Christianity, in its purest form, is nothing more than
seeing Jesus. Christian service, in its purest form,
is nothing more than imitating him who we see.
To see his Majesty and to imitate him:
that is the sum of Christianity.

—MAX LUCADO

You were created to add to life on earth,
not just take from it.

—RICK WARREN

Have thy tools ready; God will find thee work.

—CHARLES KINGSLEY

ABOUT OPTIMISM

The people whom I have seen succeed best in life have
always been cheerful and hopeful people who went
about their business with a smile on their faces.
—CHARLES KINGSLEY

It is a remarkable thing that some of the most optimistic
and enthusiastic people you will meet are those
who have been through intense suffering.
—WARREN WIERSBE

The essence of optimism is that it takes no account of
the present, but it is a source of inspiration, of vitality,
and of hope. Where others have resigned, it enables
a man to hold his head high, to claim the future
for himself, and not abandon it to his enemy.
—DIETRICH BONHOEFFER

The popular idea of faith is of a certain obstinate
optimism: the hope, tenaciously held in the face of
trouble, that the universe is fundamentally
friendly and things may get better.
—J. I. PACKER

Great hopes make great men.
—THOMAS FULLER

ABOUT TRUSTING GOD

Faith is unutterable trust in God, trust which never
dreams that he will not stand by us.

—OSWALD CHAMBERS

Faith does not eliminate problems.
Faith keeps you in a trusting relationship with God
in the midst of your problems.

—HENRY BLACKABY

Trusting God doesn't change our circumstances.
Perfect trust in him changes us.

—CHARLES SWINDOLL

God is God. He knows what he is doing.
When you can't trace his hand, trust his heart.

—MAX LUCADO

Trust in yourself and you are doomed to disappointment;
trust in money and you may have it taken from you,
but trust in God, and you are never to be
confounded in time or eternity.

—D. L. MOODY

ABOUT GOD'S GRACE

If we only believe and ask,
a full measure of God's grace is available to any of us.

—CHARLES SWINDOLL

Grace comes from the heart of a gracious God who wants
to stun you and overwhelm you with a gift you don't
deserve—salvation, adoption, a spiritual ability to use
in kingdom service, answered prayer, the church,
his presence, his wisdom, his guidance, his love.

—BILL HYBELS

We are here to be living monuments to God's grace.

—OSWALD CHAMBERS

Sin made us poor, but grace makes us rich.

—WARREN WIERSBE

The cross was heavy, the blood was real, and the price
was extravagant. It would have bankrupted you or me,
so he paid it for us. Call it simple. Call it a gift.
But don't call it easy. Call it what it is. Call it grace.

—MAX LUCADO

ABOUT THE AUTHORS

Dennis Swanberg served the local church in pastoral ministry for twenty-three years. Then, in 1995, Dennis took a leap of faith when he stepped down as church pastor and stepped up to the microphone. Soon Swan became America's Minister of Encouragement, a job he takes seriously as he continues to speak to about 150 churches and organizations every year. He has hosted two successful television series, authored eight books, and created over a dozen DVDs.

Dennis is a graduate of Baylor University, where he majored in Greek and religion (1976). He earned both a master of divinity (1980) and a doctor of ministry (1986) at Southwestern Seminary, Fort Worth, Texas.

Dennis is married to Lauree Wilkes of Fort Worth. He has two grown sons: Chad and Dusty. The Swanbergs make their home in Monroe, Louisiana.

Ron Smith is an artist manager, product developer, and business consultant. His clients have included VeggieTales, Word Music, Random House, Classic Media, and many others. Ron's company has developed more than four hundred products for retailers worldwide. He has managed Dennis Swanberg for more than a decade.

Ron is a graduate of Trevecca Nazarene University. He is married to Michelle McSpadden Smith. Together they have three children: Chase, Cole, and Carley. The family resides in Brentwood, Tennessee.

Discounts available for bulk orders of ten books or more.
Visit
TheManCode.net for additional products.
Help spread the word!

Encourage your pastor, men's ministry leader,
small group leader, friends, and family to download
the FREE sample chapter of *The ManCode*!

THEMANCODE.NET

WORTHY

If you enjoyed this book, will you consider sharing
the message with others?

- Mention the book in a Facebook post, Twitter update,
  Pinterest pin, or blog post.

- Recommend this book to those in your small group,
  book club, workplace, and classes.

- Head over to facebook.com/worthypublishing, "LIKE"
  the page and post a comment as to what you enjoyed
  the most.

- Tweet "I recommend reading #TheManCode by
  @DennisSwanberg // @worthypub"

- Pick up a copy for someone you know who would be
  challenged and encouraged by this message.

- Write a review on amazon.com, bn.com, or cbd.com.

You can subscribe to Worthy Publishing's newsletter at
worthypublishing.com.